His Excellency, Monsignor Edik Baroni

THE ARMENIAN

AND

ASSYRIAN GENOCIDE

The Coat of Arms of His Excellency Monsignor
Edik Baroni

Preface

The 20th century marked an era of genocides. Large-scale genocides began with the massacre of 1.5 million Armenians, and in the following two decades, the Nazis perpetrated the Shoah[1]. The Jewish genocide was judged at Nuremberg, but Raphael Lemkin[2], the Polish Jewish lawyer who coined the term "genocide," had already issued the warning before the Shoah: do not forget the extermination of the Armenians. Through a deliberate decades-long campaign of ethnic cleansing, Turkey uprooted its minority communities and denied their history. In the heart of the Syrian desert, approximately 450 kilometers east of Damascus, lie the ruins of the Armenian Genocide martyrs' memorial. Constructed in 1990, the memorial has long served as a pilgrimage site for thousands of

---

[1] The Holocaust, as the genocide of the Jews, is more accurately identified by the term Shoah (in Hebrew: שואה, literally 'catastrophe, destruction').

[2] Raphael Lemkin (Vaŭkavysk, June 24, 1900 – New York, August 28, 1959) was a Polish lawyer and jurist.

Armenians, descendants of a systematic genocide that once drove their ancestors into these same desert sands over a century ago. Characterized by its beige marble walls and pointed domes, the building was a splendid representation of Armenian architecture in a land where numerous members of the diaspora currently dwell. Tragically, the complex was destroyed by ISIS[3] in 2014, perhaps indicative of a cultural cleansing that was never truly resolved. The Deir ez-Zor Desert, where the Ottomans forced thousands of Armenians to march to their death from hunger or disease, is just one of the many extermination grounds used by the empire against its Christian minorities. Peter Balakian, the author of "Black Dog of Fate," reflects in his memoir on the vast number of Armenians who perished in Deir ez-Zor. During his 2009 visit to the region, he discovered that it was remarkably easy to unearth some of the victims' bones, relics of only a portion of the approximately 1.5 million Armenians who were killed by their Ottoman oppressors between 1915 and 1923. Nevertheless, despite its

---

[3] The Islamic State is an international paramilitary terrorist organization.

4

significance, the Armenian Genocide remains largely an anecdote among many in our understanding of world history. However, the aftermath of these same mass killings has significantly influenced the modern geopolitical stage and served as a harbinger of the major massacres that would follow in the 20th century. Therefore, comprehending the complexity and consequences of the Armenian Genocide is significant not only in a historical sense but also as a means of understanding the human capacity for causing harm.

Nevertheless, before delving into the magnitude of the Armenian Genocide, it is essential to grasp the historical backdrop in which it occurred.

"The attack on the Armenian people, which soon evolved into a systematic attempt to exterminate the race, was a cold-blooded, unprovoked, deliberate, meticulously planned, and executed act without popular approval, by the military rulers of Turkey."— Henry H. Riggs, an

American missionary in Kharpert during the Armenian Genocide.

If the memory of the Armenian Genocide has faded over time, the simultaneous Assyrian Genocide has likewise slipped from our collective memory. The history of the Armenian Genocide does not begin solely with the Armenians themselves. Instead, there is a broader context in which these killings commenced. In fact, it has been stated that the Armenian Genocide was not an entirely distinct occurrence but rather a part of a more extensive and prolonged genocidal policy aimed at other Christian populations as well, such as the Greeks and Assyrians. This is the argument put forth by Israeli historians Benny Morris and Dror Zeevi in their extensive book, "The Thirty Year Genocide," published in April 2019.

Christian populations in the Ottoman Empire have long played the role of second-class citizens under the rule of the Turkish Muslim elite. The Ottoman *dhimmi*[4] system afforded the Armenian Christian

---

[4] A dhimmi (in Arabic: ذمّي), plural: *ahl al-dhimma*, "People of the *dhimma*," in Turkish, *zimmi*) referred to a non-Muslim individual residing in a state ruled by

people a relatively broad degree of autonomy but also imposed upon them a different set of standards than their Muslim counterparts. In Turkish, they were already called *"giaours,"* which means "infidel" or "unbeliever," and they unfairly faced higher taxes and more stringent legal restrictions. The so-called "Armenian Question" came into debate in the late 19th century, as European powers began to take notice of the mistreatment of the Ottoman Empire toward its Christian minorities. Around the same time, Armenian leaders began receiving an increasing number of reports of crimes targeting their community, such as land seizures, forced conversions, rapes, and murders.

However, delving into the ancient Armenian culture is not limited to the examination of the genocide that took place in the early 20th century. The tragedy of the Armenian people at the hands of the Ottoman Empire and Turkey leads to the grim conclusion that it was a prolonged mass extermination that took a considerable time to be

shari'a, the Islamic legal system.

officially recognized as such. A fatalistic perspective would contend that there have always been genocides. This is undoubtedly true, but it does not authorize us to accept that this will inexorably continue to be the case throughout the rest of human history. There are a variety of causes that lead to persecutions, some of which are simply a matter of convenience to conceal other hidden agendas. Many of these causes are driven by economic motivations that ultimately lead to wars following market disputes or the need to control strategic raw materials, living space, or, as the Nazis asserted, for religious or political supremacy, or the unnatural belief in ethnic superiority.

Some genocides have been overlooked, such as the Romani Holocaust, while others have been silenced, as is the case with the Armenian Genocide. Similarly, history has neglected the enormity of certain holocausts, just as the media and multinational bodies tasked with securing world peace, particularly the League of Nations at that moment, did. The witnesses appear to have short memories, perhaps driven by the fear of being overwhelmed by such terror, which has led them to turn a blind eye.

How could the Turks, not implicated as accomplices in the genocide, watch the Armenian death caravans pass by? How could they witness men who had been hanged along the roadside? Were they not horrified to see Armenian children set ablaze like torches, or young women handed over as spoils for the harems? It raises the question, were they not engulfed by compassion? Did they not harbor the humane inclination to extend a helping hand, or offer a chunk of bread or a glass of water? Clearly not. It is probable they did not because the guilty parties had cast a pall of terror around them, capable of rendering any humanitarian response impotent.

It is imperative to adopt a position in response to such a tragedy. To prevent the recurrence of any form of mass atrocities – even as they persist– it is imperative to foster a collective awareness of respect for human life, for the lives of those around us, as it is their inalienable right.

Lemkin asked: Would mass murder be an appropriate term for such a phenomenon? How can one characterize an attempt to destroy a nation and erase its cultural identity?' He argues that the term "denationalization" is lacking because it does not emphasize biological destruction. For this very reason, terms like "Germanization" or "Italianization" are not valid because the Germans did not intend to Germanize the Jews or Poles in Western Poland; they simply wanted to annihilate them completely. However, the Turks were able to reach this objective within their territory by physically eliminating the Armenians and taking over their lands and belongings. According to Lemkin, this newly coined term, genocide, refers to "a coordinated plan consisting of various actions aimed at the destruction of the essential foundations of the life of national groups with the purpose of erasing these groups." He emphasizes that genocide is not a crime confined to one nation, rather a crime that should be of virtual concern to the entire international society. From a legal, moral, and humanitarian standpoint, it is an international crime. Cultural factors, as Lemkin contends,

10

provide the basis for international protection of national, religious, and cultural groups. Our entire heritage is the result of contributions from all nations. Lemkin astutely observed that peacetime genocide generates international tensions and eventually leads to war. "While society has predominantly focused on crimes against individuals, or more precisely, organized crimes against individuals, little has been undertaken to prevent and mete out justice for the loss of life and devastation suffered by millions of human beings." If genocide is deemed criminal because it annihilates national, racial, or religious groups, this underscores the critical importance of the international community. Once the full scope of the term genocide is defined, it is undeniable that, owing to its inherent legal, moral, and humanitarian attributes, it must be recognized as an international criminal act. This is duly acknowledged in the United Nations Charter, where it establishes the international protection of human rights and underscores that the violation of these rights by any state is a matter that concerns all of humanity. The term coined by Lemkin ceased to be merely descriptive when it was legally acknowledged that genocide is an international crime that the signatory nations of the Declaration are obligated to prevent and punish. The United Nations defines genocide as any of the following acts committed with the intent to destroy, in whole or in part, a national, ethnic, racial, or religious group as such:

• Killing members of the group

• Inflicting severe physical or mental harm upon members of the group

• Deliberately imposing living conditions on the group aimed at causing their physical destruction in whole or in part;

• Enforcing measures to prevent births within the group;

• Forced transfer of children from the group to another group. The United Nations defines genocide as the legal entity (a state, a governmental authority) that plans and carries out, or orders the execution of mass killings or intentional destruction of a national, ethnic, or religious group. By the end of 1880, there were approximately 2,500,000 Armenians residing in the Ottoman Empire. After the First World War, the number of Armenians in Turkey barely reached 100,000. This discrepancy can be attributed to the large number of Armenians who perished in massacres or were forcibly displaced to other countries between 1894 and 1921.

Los Angeles, November 1, 2023

His Excellency Monsignor Edik Baroni

The Armenians

The land of the Armenians was home to the birthplace of human civilization. Between 6000 BC and 1000 BC, archaeological evidence points to the existence of iron, copper, bronze, stone, ceramic tools and objects, along with rock inscriptions. These findings were an integral part of daily life and may have had a role in trade with neighboring lands. Armenia even appears to have been the cradle of agriculture, as carbon-14 dating tests have shown the presence of rye in the area. The mountains encircle Mount Ararat, which, according to religious scriptures, is believed to be the place where Noah's Ark came to rest after the global flood.

The first documented reference of a country by the name of Armenia can be traced back to cuneiform writings dating to the time of King Darius I of Persia (6th-5th century BC). Armenian origins flourished during the Bronze and Iron Ages. Researchers debate the influence of the Hurrians[5] on the emerging Armenia, but Armenians undeniably belong to the Indo-European group, while the Urartian kingdom[6] has its origins in the Hurrian-Urartian family. After the collapse of the Urartian kingdom, the ancient Armenian realm took its place.

Yerevan, the modern capital of Armenia, was founded in 782 BC, before Rome, by King Argishti I of Urartu. Around 600 B.C. the kingdom of Armenia was founded under the Orontid dynasty and continued through several local dynasties until the year 428 A.D. Following the destruction of the Seleucid Empire, which came after the empire of Alexander the Great, a

---

[5] The **Urrites**, commonly known as Hurrians, Khurrians, or Orrites, were a Mesopotamian population whose presence can be documented as early as the mid-third millennium B.C.

[6] The **Kingdom of Urartu** was an ancient Armenian kingdom situated between Asia Minor, Mesopotamia, and the Caucasus, centered around Lake Van (now in eastern Turkey). The kingdom lasted from 860 to 585 B.C. The name corresponds to the biblical Ararat.

Hellenistic Armenian state was established around 190 BC. After Artash, the first kings and the founder of the Artashid dynasty emerged (190 B.C.). Under the rule of the Zariadris dynasty, a new state, known as Little Armenia, achieved independence from Greater Armenia. The Kingdom of Armenia reached its peak expansion between 95 B.C. and 66 B.C. under Tigranes the Great of the Artaxiad dynasty. Influenced by contemporary empires, Armenia experienced periods of independence and autonomy. The inevitability of Armenia's position between two continents left it susceptible to invasions by Assyrians, Greeks, Romans, Byzantines, Arabs, Mongols, Persians, Turks, Ottomans, and Russians. In the year 301, Armenia became the first nation in the world to officially adopt Christianity as its religion, influenced by Saint Gregory the Illuminator, an Eastern Christian bishop who is now considered the patron saint of the Armenian Apostolic Church. Tiridates III (238-314) was the first ruler to officially propose the Christianization of his people. When the Armenian kingdom fell in 328, most of Armenia became part of the Sasanian Empire. After an

Armenian rebellion in 451, Christian Armenians retained their religious freedom, and Armenia gained autonomy along with the right to be governed by an Armenian leader, while other imperial territories were exclusively under Persian rule. The situation shifted when, in 630, the Arab caliphate vanquished the Sasanian Persia. Upon the Arab conquest, Armenia came into prominence as an autonomous principality within the Arab Empire, absorbing the Armenian lands that were formerly part of the Byzantine Empire. The principality was under the governance of the Armenian prince, recognized by both the Caliph and the Byzantine Emperor. It formed a component of the administrative division within the Emirate of Arminiyya, a creation of the Arabs, which also incorporated segments of Caucasian Georgia and Albania, with its central hub in the Armenian city of Dvin. The Armenian principality endured until 884 when it regained its independence from the weakened Arab Empire.

Armenian culture in the twentieth century

Armenian culture is one of the oldest, dating back to the third millennium BC. It remained remarkably unchanged despite Armenia's ten centuries of subjugation under the Persian Empire, the Roman Empire, the Ottoman Empire, the Russian Empire, and even as a republic within the Soviet Union. An overview of Armenian cultural life throughout the 20th century cannot overlook the challenges that impeded its development during that extended period of discrimination and oppression faced by the Armenian people at the hands of the Ottoman and Turkish regimes, especially affecting Armenian intellectuals. It is important to remember here that the initial victims of the Armenian Holocaust were cultural figures. Armenia possessed a cultural history dating back further than its existence as a nation, with understandably limited advancements during the periods of Persian and Turkish dominations. The Armenian diaspora[7] bore the duty of upholding cultural traditions from the past, while integrating the cultural advantages acquired in the countries where they could settle and develop freely.

---

[7] The term **Diaspora**, of Greek origin (derived from the Greek verb διασπείρω, meaning "to scatter"), originally refers to the "dispersion of a people across the world following their departure from their places of origin" or "the scattering of a people to various regions of the world due to the necessity of leaving their original homeland." It is also used in an extended sense to denote the "dispersion of individuals who were formerly part of a unified group.

Constantinople, India, and Venice, among other centers, served as focal points from which Armenian culture in exile radiated. The Armenian people grappled with an unceasing struggle for social freedom, and the cultural and political repercussions of this struggle were far-reaching. Politically, there has been a revival of concern for the people's way of life and a resolute pursuit of freedom from Turkish oppression, with everyone's gaze fixed on the vision of a unified Armenia.

The intellectual class of Western Armenia was influenced by Europe, especially Paris. Nevertheless, the Turks in the region refused to believe in the patriotic loyalty of Armenians, whom they considered spies or collaborators of the Russians opposing the Turks. The exacerbation of this mistrust led to the physical disappearance of Armenian intellectuals. The epicenter of Western Armenian culture lay in Constantinople and Smyrna, where educational centers embraced the principles of modern instruction but retained deep-rooted traditions that hindered modernization. Since 1886, Constantinople served as the headquarters of the

Central College, where a profusion of intellectuals, politicians, philologists, and high-level professionals in various disciplines was cultivated. The Armash Convent was established in 1889 in Izmit, a city near Constantinople. Over time, the Convent evolved into a Higher Theological School. The institution was not solely committed to religious education; it also delved into philosophical knowledge, the study of natural sciences, as well as the study of the Armenian, French, and Turkish languages. Many of their students went on to become active participants in civil life. The Turkish campaign of terror in 1915 led to the destruction of the Armash Convent and the deportation of its religious congregation members. In Aintab, there existed a three-tiered educational institution, encompassing schooling, medical education, and religious seminary. There were also Armenians in approximately 700 evangelical institutions and 500 Catholic institutions. As the Turks began their genocide, they closed Armenian schools and all national institutions affiliated with countries opposing Turkey. The slaughterhouses or orphanages were the destination for thousands of young students.

The Turks of Western Armenia were well aware and far from indifferent to those signs of what they saw as a perilous advancement. They decided to exterminate the entire Armenian population, with intellectuals among those who perished in the forefront of this genocidal atrocity.

The migration of Armenian intellectuals from prominent European cultural centers not only brought secularism but also social proposals aimed at fostering human progress, advocating for justice, and infusing a doctrinal sense into their thinly veiled revolutionary ideas. Armenian books were translated into foreign languages, while works considered classics of world literature were also translated into Armenian. Understanding the significance of this cultural wealth is essential to grasp how the Armenian people, whether with or without their land, were able to strengthen their collective memory as a means of survival in the diaspora.

The Ottoman Empire

A thorough study of the Ottoman Empire (ca. 1300-1922) is a prerequisite for a well-documented grasp of the Armenian question. The Ottoman Empire bordered Hungary to the north, Aden to the south, Algeria to the west, and Iran to the east. The territory that is now Turkey served as the center of power. The Ottoman influence spread throughout Ukraine and southern Russia. With the disappearance of the Seljuk Sultanate of Rum, a series of principalities arose, among which was the inception of the first Ottoman state. Islam contributed with its Jihad warriors[8], and the Ottomans joined them in the struggle against the Christian Byzantine Empire. The Ottoman profile

---

[8] **Jihād** is a term in the language of Islam that signifies both the effort of self-improvement by the believer (the "higher jihad"), primarily intellectual, directed, for example, towards the study and comprehension of sacred texts or law, and the war waged "for the sake of God," i.e., for the expansion of Islam beyond the borders of the Muslim world (the "lower jihad").

was progressively shaped by successes on the battlefield and the alliances forged to solidify it. They expanded to the south and east, capturing Ankara in central Anatolia and Gallipoli (Gelibolu) in the Dardanelles Strait, as they moved across southeastern Europe. Adrianople (Edirne) served as the capital, and following the Serbs' defeat in the Battle of Kosovo, they also annexed Thrace, Macedonia, a portion of Bulgaria, and Serbia. The Mongol Tamerlane (also known as Timur) defeated the Ottomans around 1402; after recovering from this setback, they expanded their power to Constantinople (Istanbul), the final Ottoman capital. They took control of territories, displacing the Iranian Safavids and the Syrian and Egyptian Mamluks, allowing them to reach the sacred lands of Arabia, the Red Sea, and the Indian Ocean. In 1534, Suleiman the Magnificent[9] incorporated Iraq into the empire, thereby gaining control of the Mediterranean via Algiers. His subsequent step

---

[9] **Solimano I**, commonly referred to as **"the Magnificent"** (to the Westerners) o"*Kanuni*" (among the Turks), also known as the Lawgiver, was born in Trebizond on November 6, 1494, and departed on September 6, 1566, in Szigetvár. He held the position of Sultan and Padishah of the Ottoman Empire from 1520 until his death.

involved advancing across Europe, aiming for Belgrade and Hungary, but he failed in his attempts against Austria. The Holy League (comprising the Papacy, Venice, and the Spanish monarchy) defeated the Imperial fleet in the Battle of Lepanto.

Military and Administration

War has played a role in conquests and has reconfigured the military as the central institutional pillar. The land grants created resources that enabled them to compensate the growing Turkish cavalry through the acquisition of additional territories. Mercenaries, slaves, prisoners of war, and Janissaries[10] contributed to the growth of the highly disciplined imperial infantry. Towards the end of the 15th century, the ranks included artillery experts and engineers. In some measure, this clarifies why there are Turks today with blue eyes, rather than almond-shaped like the Mongols.

In order to regain its splendid past, the civil bureaucracy proposed mimicking the military

---

[10] The Janissaries comprised the infantry of the Ottoman sultan's private army.

achievements of European nations. Mahmud II[11] perceived this, but the objective would have been unachievable without significant alterations in both government and society. Because while the institutional plan involved the military, modernization called for a change in structure. After abolishing the old-style army in 1831, the Sultan opted for a modern, well-paid force, educated in discipline. The bureaucracy needed to expand in order to collect taxes efficiently and establish an education system capable of producing professionally trained government officials. The expanding needs of investments in telegraph and railways necessitated substantial funds. When the state's resources could no longer suffice, it resorted to European financial dependence. As was customary then and still holds true today, financial markets exerted control and administration over the borrowed resources. Administrative centralization and a certain degree of individual liberalization (citizens' rights, greater freedoms, equal rights for Muslims and

---

[11] Mahmud II (Istanbul, July 20, 1785 – Istanbul, July 1, 1839) was the thirtieth sultan of the Ottoman Empire, reigning from 1808 until his demise.

non-Muslims) ensured that the changes had an even more profound impact.

Any reform faces opposition from various sectors that question the effectiveness of the outcomes if they are not achieved with popular support. The youth recognized as the new Ottomans are making their presence felt, demanding additional reforms, which include a Constitution that, despite being promulgated in 1876, was nullified just two years later. Nonetheless, the seed had found its footing and was beginning to sprout: renowned revolutionaries, known as the Young Turks[12], orchestrated a revolution in 1908, leading to the ousting of the totalitarian rule of Abdul Hamid II. Sultan Abdul Hamid II is not remembered in history as the son and brother of a long line of sultans, but rather for his proven inefficiency as a ruler. History will remember him as the instigator of the beginning of the fall of the Ottoman Empire and for ordering the massacre of the Armenians who were demanding just reforms.

---

[12] The Young Turks is the term used in historiography to refer to members of a late 19th-century political movement that emerged within the Ottoman Empire. Inspired by the Mazzinian Young Italy, this movement aimed to transform the then autocratic and inefficient empire into a constitutional monarchy.

His authoritarian government refused to acknowledge the basic principles of equality and respect towards ethnic minorities that had been incorporated into the initial Turkish Constitution of 1876. One of the results of the Russo-Turkish war was an influx of Caucasian and Tartar immigrants who joined forces with the Kurdish minority in dispossessing Christians of their properties and executing them without legal consequences or tolerance. In the midst of this scenario, a cultured Armenian enlightenment arrived from Tiflis, igniting the creation of revolutionary political factions. Upon Abdul's demise, the Constitution was reinstated. The revolutionaries united with the Committee of Union and Progress[13], which took over the Empire in 1903 and initiated far-reaching reforms.

The Collapse of the Ottoman Empire

The issue raised in the last century of the Empire's existence was how to make modernization satisfactory for non-Muslims while keeping the political system united. This proved impossible

---

[13] The CUP was a secret revolutionary organization in Turkey and later became the political party of the Young Turks.

because the provinces gained their autonomy (Greece, Serbia, Romania, Montenegro, Bulgaria, Moldavia) to resist the advance of the Islamists as Christian entities. Further losses followed with the separation of Macedonia, Albania, Thrace, Algeria, Tunisia, Egypt, and Libya. The Ottomans retained control over the Asian provinces and expanded their influence in Arabia. The First World War led to the rapid decline of the Empire. The collapse of the Ottomans was a result of the defeat of Allied Germany, with the situation being compounded by Russian intervention. British offensives in Iraq and Syria hastened the Empire's decline, and after the signing of the Mudros Armistice in 1918, only Anatolia remained under their control. Through the Treaty of Sèvres in 1920, the Empire relinquished its Arab provinces and faced the division of Anatolia. Mustapha Kemal[14] led an armed nationalist movement that triumphed over the Greeks in Anatolia and eastern Thrace. In 1922, the Ottoman dynasty was abolished bringing an end to a political system

---

[14] Mustafa Kemal Ataturk (Thessaloniki, May 19, 1881 - Istanbul, November 10, 1938) was a Turkish general and statesman, the founder, and the first President of Turkey (1923-1938).

that had lasted for six centuries, and in its place, the Republic of Turkey was established.

The Origins of Genocide

"Among the ranks of the Young Turks' party, a significant group promotes the idea that the Ottoman Empire should be based solely on the principles of Islam and Pan-Turkism. Non-Muslim and non-Turkish inhabitants should be forcibly Islamized (converted to Islam) and made to adopt Turkish customs, or else they should be annihilated. Such gentlemen in Turkey believe that the time has come for the implementation of this plan."

(Report from the German Vice Consul in the Ottoman Empire, Max Erwin von Scheubner-Richter).

As highlighted earlier, through various means, the ascent of nationalism converted Central and Eastern Europe into a core of sustained instability and ongoing tensions. Thus, six centuries of coexistence were shattered. Certain contemporary Turkish charges diverge from historical truth as they allude to the "Armenian betrayal," ignoring the six centuries of Turkish and Armenian coexistence within the Ottoman Empire. However, for one of its key figures, the Armenians, this coexistence did not end well. Gli armeni hanno contribuito al progresso culturale, economico e politico dell'Impero Ottomano. It must be reiterated, even at the risk of not fully grasping what transpired. The advisors to the greatest Ottoman sultans were consistently Armenians because, as the ancient inhabitants of the region, they possessed advanced strategic knowledge. The Ottoman Empire gradually lost its European territory, leading Ottoman authorities to fortify the only thing left to them: Asia Minor.

In pursuit of this objective, he conceived his Pan-Turanian plan[15], which sought to bring together a wide imperial zone of Turkic-Mongolian origin (Tajikistan, Uzbekistan, and others) into a singular territory. They were reconnecting with their profound historical beginnings. The obstacle to all of this was the area's indigenous inhabitants, the Armenians, who in the early 19th century were influenced by progressive Enlightenment ideas from Europe advocating autonomy for the Empire's populations, a model successfully adopted by countries such as Bulgaria. The Armenians were now subjected to heavy taxes, unequal treatment, constant pillaging, and an array of other hardships, but they refused to be regarded as second-class citizens in their own land. The Empire started to suppress Armenian resistance, beginning with the massacre that reached its pinnacle in the meticulously coordinated extermination plan.

---

[15] Turanism is an ideology that emerged in the 19th century, originating from Ottoman intellectuals and spreading across Turkey, Hungary, and Germany. It aimed to promote the unity and "rebirth" of all Turanic peoples, encompassing Ugro-Finnic groups, especially the Ugric peoples, Turks, and Mongols.

Although several circumstances contributed to the genocide, it is undeniable that the primary responsibility rested with the foremost heir of the Empire, the Republic of Turkey. At that time, the Empire was host to not only Turks and Armenians but also Kurds, Circassians, Assyrians, Sephardic Jews, and other groups. Some were curious to see whether the highly intelligent Armenian population would experience cultural and economic decline within the Empire. The attainment of this objective involved the combined endeavors of Sultan Abdul Hamid II, the Triumvirate[16] (Union and Progress Party), and Mustapha Kemal. The Armenian genocide occurred during a period spanning from 1880 to 1923, not to mention other repressive and disruptive actions that took place thereafter.

The anger ignited by the directive to exterminate 300,000 Armenians between 1895 and 1896 was attributed to the individual history would later dub

---

[16] Following a brief era of constitutional government, the CUP's leadership gradually transformed into a military dictatorship, with power concentrated in the hands of a triumvirate, which included Mehmed Talat Pasha, Ahmed Cemal Pasha, and Enver Pasha, the latter also serving as the Minister of War.

the Red Sultan or the Grand Assassin. His first crime was declining to support the formation of the eagerly anticipated Ottoman parliament. His brother, Murat V, had proposed this alongside the Turkish constitutionalist Midhat Pasha, the visionary behind the first Turkish Constitution in 1876. Hamid's ascension inaugurated an era of extreme authoritarianism, relentless absolutism, in which all power is centralized within a sole individual. The Turkish constitution, which had granted explicit privileges to all ethnic minorities in the Empire, was repealed, and Midhat Pasha was exiled never to return.

The Russo-Turkish War (1877-1878) led to numerous consequences that generated significant tensions among the various coexisting ethnicities within the Empire. One of these consequences was the immigration of Circassians and Tatars to the region of Anatolia. These groups, such as the Kurds, were shielded by totalitarian laws like the one famously known as the Right to Protection, which granted permission to plunder Christians. Regrettably, one of the most regressive allowances granted by Hamid's absolutism was that "every Muslim had the permission to test their saber on the neck of a Christian." The cities of Batum, Ardahan, and Kars had come under the advance of the Russian forces. The Armenians were already accused of treason for aiding the advance of the czar's troops. As a punitive measure, the Sultan encouraged Kurds, Circassians, and Tartars to create attack teams known as "Hamidiye," which were tasked with raiding Armenian residences and executing the inhabitants in case of resistance (they would later be acknowledged as paramilitary groups in the 19th century). The Russians aimed to annex the cities they had occupied to their empire, on the condition that they would duly protect the Armenian population. On March 3, 1878, the Treaty of San Stefano was formally ratified, and under Article 16 of this treaty, the Ottoman Empire committed to allowing the Russians to withdraw from the occupied territories in exchange for improvements to the provinces where Armenians resided. Months later, on July 13th, the Treaty was signed at the Congress of Berlin, but the article number was reversed, replacing 16 with 61, resulting in an ambiguous text with no real specification of improvements among the population.

Since 1885, the major Armenian political parties would come into existence overseas, all the while maintaining a significant presence within the Ottoman Empire. Prominent figures included the Armenagan Party, the Armenian Revolutionary Federation, the Hunchakian Party, and the Ramgavar Party. Resistance began to gain strength in various cities and towns, such as Zeitoun and Sasun. The Armenians responded to the Kurdish attacks ordered by the Sultan, who could no longer tolerate the fact that Armenians had connections with the outside world and with Protestantism through evangelist missionaries spread throughout Anatolia in search of new followers. Thus, around the middle of 1895, the Red Sultan ordered the massacre of Armenians throughout the Anatolia region, especially those affiliated with any political parties or religious missions.

In early 1896, the Armenians made their initial move against the Kurds in the Janasor battle, and on August 14th in Constantinople (Istanbul), a faction of Armenians took charge of the Ottoman Bank and issued a threat to detonate it unless the promised measures were fulfilled It acted as a warning bell for the Authority. The men opted against detonating the bomb, but they triggered Abdul Hamid's rage, prompting him to issue orders for additional massacres in Istanbul and the surrounding areas. Abdul Hamid's popularity across Europe and America plummeted due to the massacre of Armenians and religious missionaries sent by various powers. Simultaneously, the Prussian emperor and British businessmen were challenging the arrangement for constructing railway lines within the Ottoman Empire. There was a significant level of discontent and an insurmountable tension resulting from the territorial losses in the Balkans. In this context, a secret movement emerged in Thessaloniki (modern-day Thessaloniki, Greece), purportedly progressive and rational: The Ittihad or Young Turks Party, as mentioned in the preceding pages. His affiliations with individuals from a range of secret and diplomatic organizations in Europe and the United States would play a pivotal role in bringing about the fall of Sultan Hamid. On April

24, 1908, the entire Ottoman population, including Armenians, celebrated the change of regime, never suspecting that the destructive seed sown by Abdul Hamid II would grow exponentially under the Young Turks.

In the early 1900s, the masses were demanding constitutional rights and guarantees. Workers and peasants refused to be exploited. Similarly, the ethnic groups and minorities within the Ottoman Empire were demanding not to be treated as second-class citizens with limited rights and no guarantees. They insisted that the authorities should put an end to the ongoing violations of private property and the attacks suffered by their people. When Armenian claims grew stronger, Sultan Hamid II reacted with further massacres against Armenian cities and villages. In 1905, the Dönme community (Sefardic Jews who had converted to Islam) in Thessaloniki had cultivated secret groups with aspirations to infiltrate Istanbul and assert control over the Empire. In 1905, in Thessaloniki, the Dönme community (Sabbatean Sephardic Jews converted to Islam) had established clandestine groups aiming to infiltrate

Istanbul in an attempt to seize control of the Empire. In the meantime, the Young Turks were giving birth to the Union and Progress Party. The party was led by Ismael Enver, Minister of War; Mehmet Talaat, Minister of the Interior; and Ahmed Djemal, Minister and Governor of the Navy. The Young Turks, all members of the CUP, were closely related: Halil Mentese was an uncle of Enver and the commander of Ottoman forces, as was Nur Killigil; Jevjedt Bey was Enver's brother-in-law and the governor of Van, while Mustapha Abdul Halik Renda was Talaat's brother-in-law and the governor of Bitlis. Everyone was quite familiar with the Armenians. They were aware of the power of their intellectuals and poets, capable of organizing all types and forms of resistance, and of the courage of their men and women in defending themselves and attacking the enemy, as had been demonstrated several times within the Turkish army (the Balkan Wars). The Party promised a parliament with the participation of all the Empire's minorities. The goal was to remove the tyranny of the Red Sultan. The Armenians never hesitated to support the Young Turks in their endeavor to overthrow Abdul Hamid. In April 1909, the Young Turks dethroned the tyrant, and the party's leaders appointed Murat V, the brother of Hamid, as the new Sultan. These leaders had meticulously planned everything from the moment of their secret formation in Thessaloniki. They organized a parliamentary performance that included representatives from different fronts, including a substantial number with Armenian descents. However, the ideas of Union and Progress did not aim to foster unity and development among all the peoples of the Empire, and their actions concealed the underlying notion of the complete Turkification of all social strata within the Empire. Turkey was synonymous with Turanism and symbolized the seed of the future Armenian genocide.

There were several Turkish-origin cities aiming to restore the Ottoman Empire by establishing a common Turkish market. This endeavor, known as Pan-Turkism, had a Mediterranean outlet, with only two obstacles that could impede it: the Armenians and Russia. The Armenians could disrupt the project by gaining independence for their state and creating a geographical barrier between Turkey and the rest of the Turkic-origin peoples. This would potentially allow any adversarial power to assist in the reestablishment of an Armenian state and establish a presence in the region.

The hope of enjoying rightful civil, economic, and social rights vanished into thin air with the massacre of 30,000 Armenians in the city of Adana in 1909. Even then, there were self-defense groups that recognized the reconstitution inspired by Midhat Pasha was once again a farce. Several self-defense organizations affiliated with Armenian political parties initiated their struggle. As a result, there was a tumultuous onslaught against the Turks in 1917. With the aid of Russia, the Armenian army defeated Minister of War Enver Pasha, who resorted to genocide in the face of defeats at Mush and Sarikamish. The Turks had a secret plan against the Armenians that they would put into action when the opportunity was ripe, and unfortunately, the onset of World War I was precisely the opportunity they had been waiting for. In homage to their Mongol ancestors, the plan entailed a large-scale massacre, more organized and deadly than any recorded during the time of Sultan Hamid II. The plan was premeditated, carefully devised, methodically planned, and executed systematically. The idea of genocide had been experimented with previously, but it was formalized on August 10, 1910, at the Thessaloniki Congress. Its execution was put on hold until the impending onset of the war.

Steps before the genocide - Disarmament.

The vast majority of weapons that had been distributed to the population for the Russo-Turkish war were confiscated, and there was an intellectual decapitation of the Armenians. The first step was to execute the plan of eliminating intellectuals, politicians, poets, and religious leaders to prevent the Armenians from effectively organizing a swift defense. The abduction of over 600 intellectuals commenced on April 24, 1915, in the city of Istanbul. Every aspect was meticulously planned. Under the pretext of the Great War, all Armenians aged 15 to 45 and strong enough to wield a firearm they had never received were conscripted into the army. These soldiers were utilized solely as labor to construct trenches that would soon become their own graves. The Turks aimed to erase the Armenians and every trace of Armenian culture from the face of the earth, ensuring that there would never again be an "Armenian cause" based on territorial claims or guarantees of minority rights. The orders had been issued by the Minister of the Interior himself, Talaat, and were to be "observed without hesitation and disregarding the pangs of conscience," as stated in the chilling telegram he sent. The orders were so inhumane that some Turkish soldiers or military leaders could not believe what they had been instructed to do and sought explanations or clarifications. The response was the firing squad for anyone who refused to carry out the orders. Talaat had been very clear, "the Armenians had forfeited every right to life in the Ottoman Empire," but since ammunition could not be wasted due to the war effort, they had to be stabbed to death or drowned in the Euphrates River, among other abhorrent methods. In the cities and towns, only the sickly, teenagers, women, and the elderly would have remained.

These individuals faced the other part of the plan: deportation. In the central square of each town, a sign was hung instructing the population to embark on the "relocation." The pretext was to make the Armenians believe that they would be gathered and taken to a designated area of exclusion for their protection from the effects of the war raging in the surrounding territories. All deportation routes were meticulously planned. To the north, they would be drowned in the Black Sea; those residing in central Anatolia would be transported on foot to the Deir ez-Zor desert without food rations, where they would be thrown into natural pits and then incinerated. The methods of annihilation were truly horrifying, and, of course, neither the gender nor the age of the victims was taken into consideration. The orders issued by Talaat made it clear that not even babies in the womb were to be spared. For days, the crystal-clear waters of the Euphrates River flowed red with the blood of the bodies it washed away. Thousands of women and children ended up serving as slaves in the Pashas' harems, which is why many Turkish citizens today are unaware of their true Armenian ethnic origins.

Nothing changes for the Armenians

The plan to annihilate the Armenian people was flawless, but what prevented its full execution were the rebellious Armenian forces, comprised of both male and female volunteers, who held the Turks at bay, at least for several months, in some cities and villages. This is the reason why some were able to survive. Others managed to stay alive because they were mistaken for dead or succeeded in hiding during the deportation, or they were purchased by Arabs. Many owed their survival to Turkish or Kurdish neighbors who refused to endorse the Empire's policies, even though harboring an Armenian meant a death sentence.

The Ottoman Empire, humiliated by a shameful military defeat, is coming to an end. Greeks, French, English, and Italians temporarily divided the remnants of the Empire. Meanwhile, many Armenians began returning to their homes, never suspecting that with the resurgence of Turkey, the genocidal plan would continue Although the Young Turks were ultimately sentenced to death by the same Turks accused of organizing and carrying out the genocide against the Armenian people, the continuation of horror was already underway. While the Young Turks enjoyed their exile and false condemnation, the Turkish government was forcibly taken over by Mustapha Kemal, who meticulously pursued the genocidal plan against the Armenian people. There is something very important and noteworthy: Kemal had already joined the Party, and although he was a member who did not hide his disgust for the Triumvirate, he was explicit in expressing his antipathy toward the Armenian cause.

The Russian Revolution of 1917 fundamentally altered the landscape for the Ottoman Empire. Eastern Armenia was left vulnerable and weak against any Turkish military incursion. This provided a perfect pretext to realize the long-coveted dream of Pan-Turkism. The same did not happen with the vast western region of the ailing Empire, which was once again besieged by the Allied powers. The Armistice of Mudros was meant to bring an end to hostilities against the Empire, or rather, what remained of it. It was then that the revival began. While Armenia was in a state of confusion amid the rise of the Bolshevik

45

movement and the creation of the short-lived Transcaucasian SEIM[17], the Ottoman Empire was coming to an end. Russia and Germany signed the Treaty of Brest-Litovsk, which ceded the provinces of Ardahan, Kars, and Batum to Turkey.

The Turks wasted no time in occupying these lands, employing barbaric tactics against Armenian citizens who fought well beyond their capabilities. The Treaty of Sèvres[18] was signed in August 1920. American President Woodrow Wilson envisioned an independent Armenia containing seven of its historical provinces, granting Eastern Thrace and Smyrna to Greece. It was an announcement of the yearnings for freedom of a people who had never abandoned the struggle; the Kurdish people and a free Kurdistan were established in this Treaty signed by Turkish delegates. Yet, as they signed the treaty with their right hand, they readied their bayonets with their

---

[17] The Democratic Federal Republic of Transcaucasia, also known as the Transcaucasian Federation, was a short-lived state comprising the modern countries of Armenia, Azerbaijan, and Georgia.

[18] The Treaty of Sèvres was the peace treaty signed between the Allied powers of World War I and the Ottoman Empire on August 10, 1920, in the French town of Sèvres. In reality, this treaty was never ratified due to the opposition of Turkish nationalists and was subsequently replaced by the Treaty of Lausanne in 1923.

left. For instance, Armenia was granted seven provinces that it was supposed to repopulate. British Prime Minister Lloyd George explicitly clarified that the Allies would not continue the war solely to take territory away from the Turks; the Armenians would have to invade those lands to reclaim them. At the same time, the Turkish army was rearming and embarking on its final major offensive. The campaign was named the Armenian Campaign. It was meant to be the ultimate blow in their quest to "sweep the Armenians from the area."

The Armenians, who had placed their trust in the Allied forces, were utterly devoid of protection and engulfed in the political indifference of the great powers. It would not be absurd to ask the Standard Oil Company to elucidate the trade agreements made at that time. A pro-Sephardic Turkish government negotiating the future of Armenia alongside the foremost Anglo-Saxon oil company, even though Rockefeller[19] attempted to

---

[19] **John Davison Rockefeller** (New York, July 8, 1839 – Ormond Beach, May 23, 1937) was an American business magnate. He was a global pioneer in the oil industry, driving an unprecedented expansion. In this field, he established Standard Oil, one of the largest companies ever.

conceal it by offering substantial sums of money to Armenian refugees of that era. Wilson's popularity faded quickly, and this, along with his health issues, kept him away from the issue of Sèvres. Kemal and his army resumed their offensive. They retook Marash, Hadjin, and Urfa, among other cities. The epic valor of the Armenian cities was indescribable. They fought until their breath expired within them. In Aintab, a battle ensued with the Armenians who steadfastly refused to leave their land once more.

They held onto their motto: "Mère des Arméniens France notre espérance," unaware of the agreements the French had signed with Ankara, granting them the protectorates of Musa Dagh and the surrounding territories. Kemal confronted the city, which was renamed Gaziantep due to the "brilliant" capture (Gazy). The Turkish army completely devastated historical Armenia; they exacted revenge at Sarikamis by imprisoning or subjecting all individuals of Armenian origin to mass murder, as if they were war criminals. Military dictatorship now prevails as law, while Kemal pushed his forces westward from Ankara.

He headed towards Smyrna [Izmir], burning down the Greek and Armenian quarters before clashing with Greek forces. Though initially unsuccessful, Kemal staked everything on withdrawing his forces to the Sakarya River, where he awaited the final charge against the Greeks. The maneuver achieved its goal. It swept the entire area clean, leaving thousands of massacred bodies. His army was not new; it was the same one used by the Union and Progress Party, composed of undisciplined mercenaries, and ruthless towards any foreigners or Christians. The Allied forces stepped aside; their sole interest now was the new modern Republic of Turkey, the bridge that would connect the European powers to the oil of Baku. In 1923, the Treaty of Lausanne[20] was signed, which solidified the borders of present-day Turkey, thanks to the unwavering determination of Kemal's close friend, Ismet Pasha, who was responsible for international relations.

---

[20] The Treaty of Lausanne, known as the Lausanne Convention, is a peace treaty signed in Lausanne, Switzerland, on July 24, 1923, between Turkey and the Allied Powers that participated in both World War I and the subsequent Turkish War of Independence. The treaty brought an end to the violent Greco-Turkish conflict and reshaped the borders established by the Treaty of Sèvres, imposing new boundaries between Greece, Bulgaria, and Turkey, and putting an end to any Turkish claims on Cyprus, the Kingdom of Iraq, and Syria.

To whom does Turkey belong? Lausanne, 1923: "Turkey for the Turks!"

A few years earlier, a pro-Kurdish magazine had raised the question: to whom does Turkey belong? It listed the ethnically diverse peoples inhabiting it at the time: Greeks, Armenians, Kurds, Circassians, Nestorians, Assyrians, Tartars, Laz, etc. The article emphasized how they all celebrated festivals together at Soumela, in Trabzon. There was mutual respect among them until a rallying cry began to ignite after Lausanne in 1923: "Turkey for the Turks!" On October 29, 1923, Mustapha Kemal was elected President. Section 1, paragraph 3 of the Principles and Aims of "Atatürk" proclaimed "the respect for human rights and fundamental freedoms of all, without any distinction of race, gender, language, or religion." The Armenians had faced death and continuous persecution by the military, the Greeks in the Dardanelles alongside those from the Pontus region (Pontus meaning "sea," in this context, the Black Sea) as well as the Kurds were subject to relentless persecution during Kemal's reign until they were no longer identified as Kurds but as "mountain Turks," and the Assyrians were pushed into oblivion. However, Kemal, after his fateful use of force to accomplish his goals, began to weave a veil to conceal the carnage against the peoples who opposed his battle cry of "Turkey for the Turks." That veil still shrouds a set of taboos; it implied the Westernization of Turkey for the world. Kemal introduced the Western alphabet into schools and popular life, abandoning the previously used Arabic characters. He transformed their society by embracing modern reforms (such as banning the use of the fez, a minor restructuring easily replaced with a hat). During those years, there was also a systematic destruction of the cultural heritage of the Armenian people. There are Armenian cultural artifacts that do not feature in Turkish denialism because they pertain to tangible assets that survived the cruelest periods of the extermination. The loss of human capital is irreversible, but it is not the same story with monuments and structures – churches, mosques, chapels, fortresses, stone sculptures – which were the work of Armenian architects.

Endless Horrors

Contemporary historians ponder whether the Armenian genocide of the Turks and their Kurdish allies, among other groups, was confined to the years 1915-1918. Clearly, the genocide began before that time and reached its peak during this tragic period. If that were not the case, it would merely constitute a limited perspective of the issue, for between 1820 and 1890, the Turks were responsible for a major massacre involving nearly 100,000 souls, including Armenians, Greeks, and Bulgarians. Starting in 1894, within just two years, 300,000 Armenians were killed in Constantinople, and 30,000 in Adana. The factors that led to such a massacre included the rising Turkish chauvinism (the dream of a Greater Turkey), ethnic differences (the Turks ethnically descend from the Mongol hordes that invaded Asia Minor, hence the Turkish opposition to recognizing an Armenian state that would separate from others of the same origin), as well as their intolerance towards potential religious disparities (most Armenians are Christians, while Turks are predominantly Muslims). However, it is not true that Armenians were persecuted solely and explicitly because they were Christians, as

53

after the deportations, when they managed to settle in Islamic countries, they never encountered any issues. By the end of 1880, there were approximately 2,500,000 Armenians living in the Ottoman Empire. After the World War, the number of Armenians in Turkey was slightly over 100,000. The difference can be accounted for by the large number of Armenians massacred or forced to emigrate to other countries between 1894 and 1921. The story begins with the decline of the Ottoman Empire: the Armenians' aspiration for self-rule began to take shape with the formation of two political parties, Hnchak and Dashnaktzutiun. During this time, Sultan Abdul Hamid II, the ruler of the Ottoman Empire, was cultivating nationalist sentiments among the Turks and fostering animosity towards the Armenians among their Kurdish neighbors, aiming to surprise the revolutionaries. The initial outbreak of violence instigated by the Sultan transpired in 1894 in Sason when they rebelled against the exorbitant taxes. Thousands of people were killed by Kurdish troops, and several Armenian villages were set ablaze. Two years later, they revolted once more against Turkish autocracy, seizing the Ottoman Bank in Istanbul: 50,000 Armenians were massacred by government forces. Aided by international indifference during World War I, the Turks continued to slaughter Armenians, with mass deportations to Syria and Palestine, including Armenian soldiers serving in the Turkish Army The methods of extermination employed included starvation, physical abuse, or simply machine guns. As evident from the timeline of the Armenian genocide in this study, crushing the Armenian will to resist involved the elimination of its key thinkers. The Treaty of Sèvres was signed in 1920 between the victorious powers of World War I and the Ottoman Empire. The treaty recognized the existence of the Democratic Republic of Armenia (already an independent state since May 28, 1918), encompassing Armenian territories in Turkey and those that now constitute the Republic of Armenia. The treaty recognized the presence of the Democratic Republic of Armenia (already an independent state since May 28, 1918), which encompassed both the Armenian regions in Turkey and the territories that now make up the Republic of

Armenia. Nevertheless, he Kemalist movement did not acknowledge this treaty, which remained without effect, and the existence of the Democratic Republic of Armenia was short-lived. After 28 years of Turkish persecution, the estimated number of Armenian victims killed stands at 1.5 million people. Yet another half a million or more fled to other countries and formed communities that have reminded the world of the massacre, despite the systematic denial by the Turkish government over the years, at times pressuring global governments to downplay the massacre in an effort to save face and preserve Turkey's national identity, attributing the events to defensive measures taken in response to suspicions of an internal enemy within their borders.

The Armenian genocide, the Great Calamity, or the Armenian massacre, was the forced deportation and killing of an unspecified number of Armenian civilians, estimated at over one and a half million souls, during the rule of the Young Turks in the Ottoman Empire between 1915 and 1917, amidst the backdrop of World War I. What defined these massacres most was the brutality of those who carried them out and the use of forced marches in extreme conditions, which so often led to the death of many deportees. Other ethnic groups were also massacred by the Ottoman Empire during this period, including the Assyrians and the Pontic Greeks; some authors argue that these acts were part of the same extermination policy. The start of the genocide is commemorated on April 24, 1915, the day when Ottoman authorities arrested 250 Armenian intellectual leaders in Istanbul. Ottoman armies uprooted Armenians from their homes and forced them to march for hundreds of miles across the desert in present-day Syria, deprived of food and water. The massacres did not discriminate based on age or gender, and instances of rape and other forms of sexual abuse were distressingly common. The Ottoman Empire, which had reluctantly accepted the Treaty of San Stefano, granting independence to Romania, Serbia, and Montenegro, as well as partial autonomy to Bulgaria, was determined to prevent the establishment of an Armenian state in Eastern Anatolia, fearing it would align with Russia.

Between 1894 and 1897, the "Hamidian massacres" were carried out under Abdul Hamid II (hence their name), who was then famously referred to as the Red Sultan, as mentioned earlier. The estimated number of Armenian casualties in the Hamidian massacres, according to ethnographer William Ramsay, was approximately 200,000, though there are now many who argue it was closer to 300,000. Hamid was never directly involved in the massacres, but it was suspected that he had given them tacit approval by taking no action to stop them. Frustrated by European indifference to the killings, members of the Armenian political party Dashnaktsutyun occupied the Ottoman Bank on August 26, 1896, an incident that garnered sympathy and compassion for the Armenians in Europe and was praised by the European and American press, which referred to Hamid as "the great murderer" and "the bloody Sultan."

Certain elements within the Ottoman Empire's military, in collaboration with students of Islamic theology, attempted to restore control of the country to the Sultan and Islamic law. Disorder and conflict were rife between the reactionary forces and the CUP until the latter managed to suppress the uprising and detain opposition leaders. The movement, initially led by the emerging Young Turk government, was seen as a means to quell violence and restore order and governance. However, some sources contend that Ottoman troops took part in the plundering of Armenian enclaves in the Adana province, during which between 15,000 and 30,000 Armenians were killed. The Ottoman Empire entered World War I on October 29, 1914. By the end of that year, the government had passed compulsory military service, under which all able-bodied adult men under the age of forty-five were required to enlist in the army or pay a special tax for exemption. Under this law, the majority of men were taken away from their homes, leaving behind only women, children, and the elderly.

The Ottoman army launched an attack against Russian forces encircling the city of Kars, which was then in Russian territory. In early 1915, the Turks suffered defeat in the Battle of Sarikamis, and Russian forces under General Vorontsov launched a counterattack, pushing into Turkish territory, an area already marked by interethnic tensions between Armenians and Muslims. Numerous activists from Armenian nationalist organizations (Dashnak and Hungak) collaborated with Russian troops with the intention of launching attacks on the Ottoman Eastern Front and southeastern Anatolia. Armenian nationalist groups composed of fighters sought to establish an independent state in the easternmost part of Anatolia with the assistance of the Russians. Leveraging their shared religion and recent turmoil among Armenians within the Ottoman Empire, Russia promoted Armenian nationalism (it is worth noting that there were also Russian-Armenians within the ranks of the Tsarist army). Simultaneously, Armenians had begun advocating for the creation of an independent Armenian state. As the Russian army approached, there was an Armenian uprising against the Turks in favor of the Russians on April 20, 1915, near Lake Van, in the city of Van, where a significant number of Muslims perished, and a short-lived independent Armenian republic was established. The Russians assumed control of Van in May 1915. In August, the Russian army withdrew, and the Turks recaptured the city. In September, Van was once again seized by the Russians. Between February and April 1916, Russian forces under General Yudenich captured the cities of Erzurum and Trabzon. The Turks, led by Abdul Kerim, attempted to reclaim these cities in the summer offensive, but their troops were defeated, despite Mustapha Kemal's victories. Russia won another battle in Erzincan in July. The battles around Lake Van persisted throughout the summer and fall, with cities like Mush and Bitlis being captured and then lost again. In 1917, due to the chaos following the Russian Revolution, both sides ceased military operations in the region. The Turks redirected most of their forces southward to engage the British in Palestine and Mesopotamia. The Russian army gradually lost interest as well. By early 1918, the Russian forces in the region had virtually disappeared, and the Turkish forces easily regained all the lost territory, even crossing borders, seizing Baku in the Caspian Sea in September 1918. When the war ended, the Turks had full control of Eastern Anatolia. Enver Pasha responded to the crushing defeat in the Battle of

Sarikamis by blaming the Armenians. It was then that he ordered all Armenian recruits in the Ottoman army to be disarmed, demobilized, and sent to labor camps. Most of them were either executed or forced to work as road repairmen. Shortly thereafter, on April 24, 1915, just four days after the Van uprising, the Young Turks government believed it had to confront a nationalist popular uprising within the borders of their Empire, following the euphemistic model of Greece, Serbia, and Bulgaria. They chose to deport extensive segments of the Armenian population to southeastern Anatolia. According to Armenian sources, on the same day, the arrest of 250 Armenian intellectuals was ordered, the majority of whom were immediately executed. I followed shortly - starting from June 11, 1915 - the order to deport hundreds of thousands, perhaps even more than a million, of Armenians from all over Anatolia (except for the western coastal areas) to Mesopotamia and modern-day Syria. Many ended up in the Syrian city of Dayr az Zawr and the surrounding desert. Clearly, the Turkish government did not provide the means to protect the Armenians during their deportation or at their destination. The recruitment of most men and the arrest of hundreds of intellectuals were followed by systematic massacres throughout the Empire. In Van, Governor Djevdet Bey ordered irregular troops to commit crimes and force the Armenians into rebellion, thereby justifying the Ottoman army's siege of the city, as recounted by the Venezuelan mercenary Nogales, who served in the Turkish army. ordered that all Armenian males in the city be assassinated. The Turks believed that what was happening in Van was simply an Armenian uprising being quelled by Ottoman forces during those days. It is estimated that there were approximately twenty-six concentration camps to confine the Armenian population (Dayr az-Zawr, Ra's al-'Ain, Bonzanti, Mamoura, Intili, Islahiye, Radjo, Katma, Karlik, Azaz, Akhterim, Mounboudji, Bab, Tefridje, Lale, Meskene, Sebil, Dipsi, Abouharar, Hamam, Sebka, Marat, Souvar, Hama, Horns, and Kahdem), located near the Syrian and Iraqi borders. Some Armenian sources argue that some of these may have served as nothing more than mass gravesites and other detention centers where they succumbed to epidemics and starvation. The

British occupying force actively engaged in wartime counterpropaganda efforts (during World War I, the Ottoman Empire fought as part of the "Central Powers" coalition, alongside Austria-Hungary, Germany, and Bulgaria). For instance, Eitan Belkind was a British spy affiliated with Nili (the Jewish espionage network that supported Britain against the Ottoman Empire during World War I), who infiltrated the Ottoman army as a government official. He worked at Hamal Pasha's central office. He swore to have witnessed the incineration of five thousand Armenians in a camp not far from his residence. As mentioned earlier, between April 24 and 25, 1915, many prominent figures, including writers, poets, lawyers, doctors, priests, and politicians, were arrested, deported, and subsequently put to death in the following months. In a secret session held in January 1915, the Young Turks decided to: 1. Based on Articles 3 and 4 of the Committee of Union and Progress, dissolve all Armenian associations, arrest Armenians who had ever worked against the government, send them to provinces like Baghdad or Mosul, and eliminate them along the way or upon arrival. 2. Confiscate any weapons. Inflame Muslim sentiment using appropriately tailored means in districts such as Van, Erzurum, or Adana, where the Armenians had indeed stirred up Muslim hatred and incited organized massacres. 4. Exploit the population of provinces like Erzurum, Van, Mamuret-ul-Azzis, and Bitlis, and deploy military law enforcement forces (such as the gendarmerie) only to make it appear as though they were attempting to halt the killings; these same forces would be actually needed to actively assist Muslims in areas like Adana, Sivas, Bursa, Ismit, and Smyrna. 5. Implement measures to exterminate Armenian males under the age of 50, priests, and teachers; allow young people and children to convert to Islam. 6. Deport the families of those who had fled and take actions to sever all communication with their hometown. 7. Assert that Armenian officials could be spies, remove them, and completely exclude them from any significant position or service in the state administration. 8 The task of efficiently eliminating the Armenian soldiers falls upon the military. 9. Carry out the operation simultaneously across the entire territory to prevent them from taking defensive measures. 10. Keep these instructions strictly confidential so that only two or three individuals are aware of them.

The American Ambassador to Turkey, Henry Morgenthau, confidentially reported to his country's authorities, which were still neutral, the extent of the genocide in a document that was declassified after the end of the war. In "The Murder of a Nation," Morgenthau outlines the genocidal strategy: first, the mobilization of Armenian men "fit for battle" into the Turkish army's service; then, the rapid stripping of their military status, disarmament, and the denial of their civil rights. They were consigned to labor under extreme conditions, building roads and railways, where they suffered physical punishments from their supervisors. Hundreds of thousands perished under these conditions of forced labor, starvation, disease, as they never received any medical assistance, and due to a life exposed to the elements without protection from the winter snow and scorching sun in the summer. They would all be stripped of the few possessions they had managed to hold onto, and eventually, all survivors who had not completely exhausted their strength through grueling work would be eliminated once they were completely devoid of clothing. After the extermination of the young men who had been mobilized into the armed forces, the remaining male population would be imprisoned and ruthlessly massacred. Morgenthau recounts how the killers further intensified their suffering by forcing them to dig their own graves before being shot. He describes an incident that occurred in July 1915. In the city of Harpoot, two thousand former soldiers were taken away to perform roadwork. Knowing that many had died doing this labor, the women of the town pleaded for mercy with the military leader. He not only pledged to spare the lives of these two thousand Armenians but also reiterated this commitment before the religious authorities of the region. Then, betraying every promise made, nearly all of them were mercilessly slaughtered, and the few survivors who managed to escape bore public witness to the atrocities they had endured. Another two thousand young men followed the same path, and to prevent potential escapees from being deprived of the strength needed to flee, they were starved before the Kurds were ordered to massacre them. This clear death sentence for the young was aimed at ensuring that no one would be capable of resisting, rebelling, or, naturally, reproducing. Inevitably, however, there were survivors; men who managed to evade this murderous conscription by going into hiding. Others had been promised exile, but when they departed in groups of four, of all ages, they found themselves in death caravans where they were ruthlessly killed with axes and knives to save the cost of bullets and ammunition. The entire male population of Angora (Ankara) between the ages of fifteen and sixty was first stripped of all their possessions, castrated to ensure they could never procreate, and ultimately wiped out, with their bodies left to be scavenged by vultures. For both Morgenthau and Toynbee, the fate of women had multiple tragic dimensions. Younger women were enslaved in Turkish households, while others were compelled to become part of harems, also subjected to slavery. Women deemed unacceptable were either bayoneted or thrown off cliffs. Thirst, hunger, sunburns, diseases, and madness were the fate of those they ordered to march, who were then killed wherever they fell, reduced to mere exhausted skeletons. Those who survived the death marches arrived in the camps of Syria and Iraq in conditions unrecognizable as human.

The trial against the Turkish genocides, which was by no means a real trial

With the end of the First World War, the new administration needed to present an international image entirely separate from the atrocities committed against the Armenian population by the Young Turks, other members of the Central Committee of the Union and Progress Party, and provincial administrators directly responsible for the genocide. Most of the key culprits suspiciously managed to find the time to evade legal action and escape from Turkey They were tried in absentia, and some were sentenced to the death penalty. Attempts to freeze their financial assets failed because, although they did not act clandestinely – as they were part of the repressive government – their accounts were held by proxies who were impossible to trace, as is often the case in modern times with dictators. The Young Turks were convicted because their guilt could not be denied, but in the end, they not only eluded the feeble grasp of justice but also had their sentences commuted by Mustapha Kemal, and many of them returned to be part of those who continued the extermination. Talaat was assassinated in March 1921 by Soghomon Tehlirian, a member of the Armenian Revolutionary Federation (Dashnak). On Hardenberg Strasse in Berlin, Soghomon drew a pistol and shot Talaat in the head. Shocked onlookers, unaware of the tragedy behind his action, subjected him to a beating that was later repeated at the police stations. In broken German, Tehlirian simply tried to explain, "I am Armenian, he is Turkish, I mean no harm to Germany," but his limited command of the language was inadequate to convey that it was an act of revenge against Talaat, who had ordered the massacre of his entire family in the village where they lived. Talaat was buried in the Turkish cemetery in Berlin. In 1943, his remains were transferred with full honors to Istanbul and reinterred in Sisli. Once again, historical amnesia prevailed.

Nothing has changed with Mustafa Kemal

We must, therefore, understand if genocide is compatible with modernity. Mustafa Kemal proclaimed the independence of the Republic of Turkey and promised a Europeanized country. His main achievements, while not insufficient, included the abolition of the sultanate, the establishment of monogamy, a secular educational and legal system, and the introduction of the Gregorian calendar and the Latin alphabet. Quite notably, he banned the use of the popular fez as a head covering. Do these reformist measures suffice to recognize that a nation has achieved modernity? A society is deemed modern when the rule of law is upheld, individuals can democratically express themselves through their representatives, justice is impartial, state resources are utilized to ensure the well-being, housing, and decent employment of its citizens, and there is no discrimination of any kind (ethnic, religious, human, or political). Modernization is considered complete when a country achieves scientific and industrial development, generating prosperity for its people and a developed economy for peace.

There is no doubt that he introduced reforms inspired by Western experiences, but he unequivocally participated in the atrocities that led to the extermination of 1.5 million Armenians and gave rise to other genocides in the 20th and 21st centuries. And it was he who continued with these atrocities. When he faced the Constantinople Military Tribunal on January 28, 1919, during the trials initiated against the genocides, he attempted to conceal his involvement in the extermination by lying about his past. His biography reveals a shadowy figure, one who can hardly be seen as sowing the seeds of a modern, law-governed state, when the entire world knows that the Turkish Republic usurped Armenian territories and set in motion the genocide. This is one of the reasons why Turkey should be subjected not to photographs but to X-rays, to reveal the millions of corpses that were never given a proper burial, crying out to the world for justice, plain and simple justice, and nothing but justice. The defeat of the Turkish Empire in the First World War created the conditions for Mustapha Kemal - then a high-ranking officer of the defeated expansionist army - to discover political talents that allowed him to negotiate with both Lenin and France and England, pledging to rise above the remnants of the Empire and establish a republic on that basis. Mustapha Kemal and his supporters are responsible for: 1) The extermination of Armenian populations in Cilicia and the desecration of their temples and monuments; 2) The burning and destruction of Smyrna in September 1922, where hundreds of thousands of Greeks and Armenians lost their lives; 3) The historical vindication of Talaat, the chief perpetrator of the Armenian genocide. Talaat, the genocidal murderer assassinated on the streets of Berlin in 1921, whose remains were returned to Turkey by Hitler in 1943. Today, Talaat has a mausoleum in Sisli, Istanbul, on Hurriyet Hill (Hill of Eternal Freedom). On the 60th anniversary of his death, he received official honors. Could one imagine a monument to Eichmann or Himmler in Germany or to someone like Videla in Argentina? 4) Nullify the sentences imposed by a Turkish tribunal (1919) on the officers responsible for the Armenian killings; 5) The forced enslavement of over a hundred thousand Armenian children and girls, orphaned by the genocide, in Turkish harems, and the forced Turkification of Armenian children in special schools where they were stripped of their identity. Mustapha Kemal entrusted this task to the activist and "identity converter" by the name of Halide Edib Adivar: 6) The massacre and deportations of the Kurdish people from 1923 to the present day, reaching its peak in 1926; 7) Disregarding the obligations undertaken in the controversial Treaty of Lausanne (1923) concerning the minorities living in what is now Turkish territory (Armenians were the majority population in these territories before the genocide); 8) Enforcing Section 301 of the Penal Code (punishing any direct or indirect reference to the genocide).

Erosion of Memory

When does a genocide become forgotten? In "The Armenian Genocide, Memory, Politics, and Future," historian Roger Smith discusses the erosion of memory to describe how the Armenian Genocide, despite being widely acknowledged at the time it occurred due to the abundance of news in newspapers, books, articles, official

74

investigations, eyewitness accounts, and the trial of the perpetrators in Constantinople in 1919, was silenced within a few years by external forces beyond the Armenian community. What are the causes that lead to this "erosion" of memory? A first answer would be that countries, groups, or individuals have short memories regarding events that do not directly concern them. Another explanation can be found by considering the stages through which this oblivion has passed. With the Treaty of Lausanne (1923) and the establishment of the Republic of Turkey, Armenia ceased to exist as an independent state, and Armenians ceased to make headlines. A small part of Armenia, which was established as an independent country between May 28, 1918, and December 2, 1920, was Sovietized, meaning there was no state to claim its victims. The Second World War and the Holocaust diverted the world's attention from the challenging Armenian situation, while Turkey simultaneously pursued a policy of concealment, distortion of history, and denial. The United Nations Convention agreed with the Jewish-Polish jurist Raphael Lemkin in referring to the Holocaust perpetrated by the

Nazis as "genocide." The United Nations Convention on genocide provided the international legal framework to ensure that crimes against vulnerable groups would not go unpunished. No one could argue that punishment for a state of genocide should entail interference in their internal affairs. Before the advent of Nazism, Lemkin had expressed his concern about the victimization of Armenians who could not seek justice for reparation, emphasizing that without a legally regulated international framework, if the Turkish genocidaire Talaat had not been assassinated by a member of the Armenian resistance, he could have evaded punishment for his crimes by appealing to the respect for Turkish sovereignty. The Armenian Genocide and the Jewish Holocaust are to some extent interconnected. The Armenian tragedy foreshadowed the Jewish tragedy; it was the precursor to the Holocaust. "The Armenian Genocide was the dress rehearsal for the Holocaust" (Leo Kuper and Israel W. Chasny). "Nothing emboldens a criminal more than the knowledge that he can commit a crime with impunity. This was the message conveyed to the

Nazis for not bringing the Armenian massacre to trial" (David Matas, Canadian international law expert). Hitler believed that the destruction of a particular group or nation, no matter how criminal the act, is likely to be accepted in one way or another, provided it is accompanied by a certain degree of success, because "the world believes only in success" (Documents on British Foreign Policy).

Turkish Denialism

The Republic of Turkey, the successor to the Ottoman Empire, does not deny that the massacres of Armenian civilians indeed occurred but argues that it was not a genocide because the deaths were not the result of a mass extermination plan ordered by the Ottoman state but rather a result of interethnic strife, diseases, and starvation during the upheavals of the First World War. However, scholars, including some Turks, consider the events suitable for the current definition of genocide. The events involving the Armenians are typically acknowledged as the inaugural instance of a systematically organized modern genocide. Indeed, it stands as one of the most extensively documented genocides, second only to the Holocaust against the Jewish people, among other victims of the Nazis. In 1914, before the eruption of the First World War, a substantial Armenian population resided within the Ottoman Empire, although there exists some debate regarding the precise figures. According to the report provided by the Armenian commission at the Congress of Berlin, in 1878, the figure was 3,000,000. Similarly, in 1867, Ottoman authorities mentioned the existence of a population of 2,400,000 Armenians within the country's borders, although after the Treaty of San Stefano, when the Armenian issue began to be seen as a problem for the Empire, the Turks reduced this number to between 1,160,000 and 1,300,000. Other estimates range between 1,325,000 (the lowest figure) and 2,100,000 (the highest). While primarily concentrated in eastern Anatolia, there was also a significant Armenian community in the west, particularly in the capital, Istanbul, where there is still a substantial Armenian minority today.

In her study "The Armenians – Portraits of Hope," Huberta von Voss argues that denialism is the internationally recognized term to describe the stance of the Turkish state and society towards the Armenian genocide. She notes a distinction, however, in the appropriate use of the term, asserting that it is accurately applied to the Turkish state but interpreting its lack of resonance within Turkish society as a result of ignorance, apathy, and silence. Von Voss accuses Turkey of suffering from a lack of historical awareness, a country experiencing social amnesia, unable to remember its past. The Turkish state has implemented a nationalist version of history in its educational system, resulting in a striking lack of awareness regarding the transition from the Ottoman Empire to the Republic of Turkey. According to Huberta von Voss, the official version not only ignored or distorted the Armenian genocide but also the history of other ethnic and religious minorities. The result is a deliberate collective amnesia instilled by the Turkish government? It could be. The alphabet reform in 1928, replacing Arabic script with Latin script, allowed the state to "purify" history and prevent society from accessing its own past, as only government-approved texts were transcribed. Turkish society lacks genuine access to its own past. In situations of this nature, Powers often resort to concealment tactics, claiming "not to know." This is what some German sectors did after World War II, and it was also a recourse employed by those seeking to mask the multitude of deaths that occurred during the military dictatorship in Argentina in '76. What is publicly stated is: "The Armenians got what they deserved for aligning with the Russians against the Turks," but in private, many sectors of Turkish society do not actively endorse denialist policies. It is precisely because the past has been kept hidden that Turkish society has made no contribution to helping clarify the conflict. This is what must change, von Voss argues. The Turkish state can no longer suppress discussion of its past because, whether one likes it or not, that past exists, just like the social and economic classes, the mountain Kurds, and various ethnic, religious, and cultural groups.

Building upon the Turkish denialism argument, as advocated by Huberta von Voss, she interprets the reason why Armenians place such great importance on Turkish recognition of the genocide. They have various reasons. It is widely known that victims of such human catastrophes undergo a "second traumatization" when their original suffering goes unrecognized. Ciò rappresenta anche una minaccia per l'identità armena nella diaspora. This also poses a threat to the Armenian identity in the diaspora. The Turkish government continues to deny that a century ago their predecessors exterminated 1.5 million Armenians. Furthermore, as can be seen elsewhere in this study, Article 301 of the Penal Code is still enforced against anyone publicly mentioning or writing about the massacre. Persistent claims by countries to denounce the massacre led the Turks to cancel the purchase of a spy satellite in 2001 because the French National Assembly declared the killing of Armenians as genocide. Furthermore, as can be seen elsewhere in this study, Article 301 of the Penal Code is still applied to anyone who publicly mentions or writes about the genocide. The persistent claims of countries to denounce the genocide led the Turks to cancel the purchase of a spy satellite in 2001 because the French National Assembly declared the killing of Armenians a genocide.

At a Holocaust Congress held in Philadelphia in the year 2000, researchers from around the world, including Israeli historians, signed a public declaration affirming the reality of the Armenian genocide, and in 1997, a meeting of the International Association of Genocide Scholars voted in favor of a resolution acknowledging that Armenians were victims of a large-scale genocide.

The influence of Turkish lobbies in the United States.

In the year 2000, the United States Congress drafted a bill on the Armenian genocide, requesting that President Clinton refer to the killings as genocide in his annual address commemorating Armenia. Turkey threatened to close American air bases in the country and cancel arms purchase orders from the United States. President Clinton, of course, did not use the term genocide.

"The Armenians have been the target of a genocide campaign, a heinous crime in a century marked by bloody crimes against humanity. If I am elected president, I will ensure that our country adequately acknowledges the tragic suffering of the Armenian people," was GW Bush's response during his presidential campaign to a question from the Armenian community about his policy regarding the genocide if elected. Once he assumed the presidency of the United States in 2001, Bush no longer used the word genocide but rather "infamous killings" and a "tragedy that marked the history of the Armenian people and their bitter fate at the end of the Ottoman Empire." Twenty-nine countries and forty-two U.S. states had passed (as of November 2019) a formal resolution recognizing the Armenian genocide as a historical event.

Genocide of Christians

Lemkin considered eight social conditions conducive to genocide and referred to thirteen techniques, whose preparation could serve as a warning that genocide was beginning. The conditions included religious or racial fanaticism, irredentism concerning changes in national borders, social or political unrest, economic exploitation, colonialism, or militarism aimed at conquest, proximity of the victim group, genocidal ideology by the perpetrator, and contempt for the victims, along with circumstances contributing to the vulnerability of the victim group. The techniques included massacre, mutilation, deprivation of the necessities of life, enslavement, family separation, sterilization, abortion, destruction of cultural treasures, looting, destruction of religious sites, prohibition of religious rituals or other group activities, forced conversion, and demoralization. All these conditions and techniques occurred in the Assyrian case. Firstly, religious and racial fanaticism prevailed under Ottoman rule and resurged in 1911-1914. Pan-Islamism, a mindset rooted in the idea of a global war between Muslims and pagans or other monotheists, coalesced into a more organized and recognized political movement between the late 19th and early 20th centuries. Abdul Hamid assumed the sultanate in 1876 and eventually earned the nickname the "Red Sultan." Si circondò di dignitari religiosi, li reintegrava nell'élite politica e adottò una retorica panislamica, facendo appello alla solidarietà musulmana sia in materia interna che esterna." He surrounded himself with religious dignitaries, reinstated them in the political elite, and adopted a pan-Islamic rhetoric, appealing to Muslim solidarity both domestically and internationally. The Associated Press reported in May 1895 on "indications that the Sultan has put plans into motion for the systematic persecution of Christians in all parts of the empire." One method, for example, was to starve the independent Assyrians in the region between Mosul and Lake Van. Most of the Christian clergy had been killed in dozens of villages. Although the transition from this Sultan to the CUP is often described as a regime change from pan-Islamism to secular progressivism, religious fanaticism did not disappear in the era of the "Young Turks." In a 1910 meeting, the CUP discussed how the Assyrians "stubbornly resist every attempt to Ottomanize them," so that "all these efforts must inevitably fail." A CUP leadership meeting in 1911 discussed the Empire's Christian subjects as a problem. CUP intellectuals regarded Genghis Khan and Tamerlane, perpetrators of widespread massacres, as somewhat of role models. The removal of "non-Turks" from Anatolia was decided upon. Ziya Gökalp, a member of the Young Turk regime from 1911 to 1918, advocated for the creation of a nation unified by religion and established the foundational narrative of modern Turkey, which posited that there had been betrayal by minorities against the Turks, akin to the Nazi ideology of a Jewish "stab in the back" in 1918. Instead of being a wartime crime of passion, the massacre policies emerged along a continuum. Even prior to World War I, the Ottoman Empire shared the Prussian ideal of "absolute war," the type of non-chivalrous population-based extermination campaign that later evolved into "total war." German geopolitical theorists advised the Ottomans to operate "without any sentimentality towards all nationalities and ethnicities in Turkey that did not align with Turkish plans." U.S. Ambassador Henry Morgenthau explained the German-Ottoman strategy in the aftermath of the Balkan Wars when the Russo-Ottoman conflict reignited: to ruthlessly eliminate minority populations like Armenians, Greeks, Assyrians, and other Christians, and populate their territories with Muslim Turks to prevent a recurrence of the "Bulgarian problem." In other words, "making Turkey exclusively the land of Turks." The strategy was likely implemented during the massacres of around 20,000-30,000 Armenians in Cilicia in 1909, as a case of incremental resort to religious cleansing and forced conversion. The entire Christian population of Adana, other parts of Cilicia, Aintab, and Marash faced harsh measures in 1909, after which the CUP embraced the doctrine of Turkism, asserting that the empire must be of exclusively Turkish descent to thwart powers intervening on behalf of their Christian co-religionists. In 1911, the CUP initiated the planning for the deportation of the Empire's Christian subjects. Preparations for the Armenian and Assyrian massacres were set in motion during secret meetings in Erzurum in 1913. The CUP appointed ultra-nationalist extremists to governorships in Eastern Anatolia in 1913. Deliberate arson and widespread looting against Armenians and Assyrians began in August 1914, before the Ottomans joined the war by attacking Russia. The destruction of Christian life in the Ottoman Empire began long before the war, as early as 1890, and continued under Mustafa Kemal after 1918. This trend, along with attacks on unarmed Armenian and Assyrian civilians in Albaq, near Başkale, before the war and in many other places during the war, contradicts the implication made by Anzerlioğlu, Özdemir, Sonyel, and Wilmshurst that if the Chaldeans and Nestorians had remained neutral, as they could have, they would have been spared from the genocide. In November 1915, the Austro-Hungarian Ambassador Pallavicini confirmed that Talât Pasha, the Ottoman Minister of Interior, had acknowledged that his plan was to "eradicate foreign elements" in Anatolia. The New York Times reported the statement of this minister that "there was no place for Christians in Turkey." In July 1915, the German consul in Samsun wrote that: "It is a steadfast principle of the present rulers to convert all of Turkey to Islam and employ any available means to achieve it." He predicted that none of the victims would survive. A holy war was declared. A document stated that "the blood of infidels in Islamic lands may be shed with impunity, except for those to whom Muslim power has promised security and who are allied with it," the latter exception being applicable to Germans and Austro-Hungarians. The CUP elevated an enthusiast of such bloodshed, Dr. Mehmed Reşhid, to the position of governor in Diyarbakir and appointed him to rule over the entire southeastern expanse of Anatolia. Also in 1922, Mustafa Kemal led the jihad-i milliye or national holy war of the Turks against Britain, Greece, and the surviving indigenous

Christians; the French sided with him after the massacre of the French garrison in Urfa in 1921, and even the Russians, under Lenin and Stalin, supported him. Former proponents of Ottoman aggression and extermination policies rallied behind the Kemalist cause in 1919-1920. The Kemalists prohibited the distribution of food or blankets in charity to many Christians, particularly the Assyrians. The rationale was that "the Assyrians were enemies of the government and should be killed." Mustafa Kemal proclaimed in 1922 that more "massacres" were on the way. George Horton, the U.S. consul in the Near East, believed him. Secondly, irredentism and the desire to expand Ottoman territory were pressing matters. In a disquieting preview of some of the major battles of World War II, Ottoman War Minister Enver Pasha's plan to annex territory from the Russian Empire involved seizing the Baku oil fields and advancing into the rest of the Caucasus, Afghanistan, and India. The official declaration from the CUP to its regional commanders was that the Turkish race would unite for the "destruction" of the Russians. When discussing atrocities against the Greeks, Turkish officials, sympathetic journalists, and scholars almost always mention "Greek irredentism," even though this term is rarely used for Turkish nationalists, pan-Turks, pan-Islamists, or other national or religious leaders in the Middle East during the early 20th century. Panslavism is also frequently accused, with claims that Russians or Slavs conquered the Caucasus in general or Circassia in particular and displaced the indigenous Muslim or Turkish inhabitants. However, Georgians were indigenous there before Turkish, Arab Muslims, and Seljuk conquests. Similar to the Germanic conquests that led to the German exodus when they collapsed, massacres, enslavement, and pillaging of the civilian population were widespread when Georgia and eastern Armenia fell into Seljuk hands. Social and political turmoil reached its zenith in the spring and summer of 1915. As early as August 1914, the United States Ambassador to the Ottoman Empire, Henry Morgenthau, predicted an "imminent" massacre of Christians following the Ottoman and their allies' declaration of war against the Russians and their allies. In March 1915, the governor of the province of Van accused the Armenians of insulting Islam by allegedly "attacking the world of Islam, converting mosques into stables, forcing students to embrace Christianity, uttering obscene insults, assaulting the religion," and other acts of "treason." By July, some Ottomans had leveled wide-ranging allegations of an "Armenian and Assyrian conspiracy" to unite with the Russians, asserting that, in order to quell the "revolutionary movement," all Armenians and Assyrians must depart. The Ottomans had suffered 70,000 casualties, including at least 33,000 fatalities in the campaign against the Russian Empire to the east, and 86,000 deaths, with 10,000 killed or wounded on just May 19, in the campaign against the British Empire to the west. In 1916, Talât Pasha admitted that the "security of Turkey" had taken precedence over humanitarian concerns, as "serious excesses" had occurred during the deportations. Ottoman leaders regarded the Assyrians and Christian communities as a fifth column that could potentially assist Russia or the Western European powers, much like how Hitler and the Nazis viewed Jews as a fifth column that could aid Britain, America, the Soviet Union, and global anti-Nazi efforts. Some German observers, allies of the Ottoman Turks, reflected and at times encouraged this perception of a crisis involving Christian uprisings. A renowned German expert on Turkey, Baron Max von Oppenheim, noted that Armenians and Assyrians had become "openly hostile" towards the Turks and that "if the [British] enemy lands [in Turkey], the Christians would join forces with the enemy to foment a rebellion." Economic exploitation intensified between 1890 and 1910. After months of expropriations in 1895, "no official declaration condemned the practice of killing and robbing Armenians and Assyrians wherever they were encountered." In 1896, the United Press reported that nearly all Christian areas in the Bitlis province had been plundered. In the city of Harput in 1896, there was "a large crowd of hungry and trembling men, women, and children who had experienced similar ordeals of fleeing barefoot and sleeping amidst the ruins of the Christian neighborhood." At the outset of World War I, the Ottoman Empire deported the Greeks from Thrace and northwestern Anatolia, reallocating their homes and properties to refugees from the Balkan wars or conflicts involving Russia and Turkish peoples. The Christians deported to the interior of Anatolia for service in labor battalions were, in fact, reduced to slavery, denied food and shoes, tortured, and killed by the tens or hundreds of thousands. In 1918, a German diplomatic report stated that by the end of 1917, the Ottoman Empire had conscripted over 200,000 Greeks into the army and labor battalions, many of whom perished due to brutal treatment, starvation, disease, and exposure to the cold. The Ottomans had a long tradition of colonialism and militarism aimed at conquest, and the Young Turks developed a new and virulent strain of this aggressive ideology. According to the CUP, a caliph would rule from Africa to India. Armenian historian Tigran Matsoyan reveals pervasive similarities between the Armenian Genocide and the Holocaust, including pan-Germanic and pan-Turkic ideologies and propaganda; the mass burning, drowning, or starvation of victims; and the acceptance of bribes to prevent deportation and avoid certain death. An "extreme wing of the CUP'" hoped to establish "a new society based on a singular ethnic-religious, linguistic, and cultural identity." At the Young Turks (CUP) conference in Thessaloniki in 1908, its leaders had deliberated and reached an agreement to pursue the "complete Ottomanization of all Turkish subjects." This was not strictly necessary to the extent that the subjects of the Turkish Sultan were already Ottoman subjects. The discussion might have revolved around the elimination of international treaty protections for Ottoman Christian subjects, which led to international inspections of sites where Armenians and Assyrians had been massacred and deported from their homes by Kurdish tribes and Ottoman officials. Apparently, Talât announced at the Thessaloniki conference that "equality" before the law would first require the "Ottomanization of the Empire." The verb "Ottomanize" evokes what Lemkin referred to as "Germanization" or 'the imposition by a stronger nation (Germany, Hungary, Italy) of its national model on a controlled national group." He labeled this imposition as a genocide, or a "policy of imposing a national model," utilizing "a system of colonization." In the Ottoman case, the CUP mobilized a 'Special Organization with the aim of destroying and annihilating Armenians and Assyrians' and equipped "butcher units" within the Ottoman Third Army, particularly in Harput but also in Bitlis, Diyarbakir, Erzurum, Sivas, Trabzon, and Van. As in other genocides, where proximity made the victim group vulnerable, the Assyrians lived among the Turkish, Kurdish, and Persian peoples who would contribute to the genocide, while they lacked strategic depth or an outlet to the sea or another land to draw upon. Furthermore, this proximity existed under circumstances that ensured the weakness of Assyrian defenses. After the fall of Nineveh and later Babylon, Assyria became a province, at times a kingdom, within other empires. Greeks, Persians, Arabs, and Romans acknowledged that Assyria was still a region in their geographical literature. Assyria's homeland was situated along major trade routes in the late Middle Ages and modern times, spanning a route from Ankara, Izmir, Aleppo, and westward towards Mosul, Baghdad, Susa, and eastward, encompassing Harran, the plain of Nineveh, Merdā (Mardin), Nṣībīn (Nisibin) [Turkish: Nusaybin], Edessa, and Pesh-khabour/Faysh Khabur). Mount Izla, near Mardin, is referenced in ancient Assyria and texts as İzela. Some Assyrians sought refuge in Mount Izla, or the "mountains of Izlo," after the fall of the Assyrian empire. The ancient Assyrians referred to the Tur Abdin region as "Nirbu" and its mountains as 'Kaşiari' (Kashiari daglari). It is situated southeast of Diyarbakir, northeast of Edessa, northwest of Nisibin, and southwest of Midyat. In order to expand their control and suppress rival nationalities, the Ottomans and their Kurdish allies employed massacre, family separation, and deprivation of the essentials for life. Moreover, mutilations, enslavement, plunder, devastation of cultural and religious treasures, restrictions on minority religions, and forced conversions occurred. In the nineteenth century, the Assyrian patriarch sought help from the Russian Empire, as his flock was enduring the "constant" abduction of Assyrian girls and women. Meanwhile, Turkish and Kurdish landowners demanded "unpaid labor" and seized wheat from Assyrian farmers. A British agent reported that the Turks "hated" the "Christian population, believing it to be one of the main causes of the [Russo-Turkish] war and the resulting misfortunes of Turkey." The English received reports that the Sultan "feared that an active and intelligent Christian population might seek freedom as the Bulgarians had done, and which they achieved through Russia's hand in 1878." In 1896, German activist Johannes Lepsius conducted an investigation into Christian areas in Turkey and asserted that 1,100 churches and monasteries had been damaged or razed due to violence, and that 546,000 people had been reduced to poverty due to the destruction of their homes, villages, and livelihoods. In 1915, Ottoman forces gathered Assyrians and other Christian men in the Diyarbakir area, executed them, abused women, and laid waste to Assyrian towns. A British administrator in the former Ottoman province of Mosul described how, during the war, Kurdish bands captured Assyrian women, leading many to their deaths in a harsh terrain while plundering Assyrian homes and religious buildings. The Near East Relief Foundation reported on the conditions of these refugees, as well as those displaced in Persia: virtually all of their household belongings and food supplies had been plundered; the same was true for their livestock, upon which they heavily relied for sustenance; their homes lacked doors and windows, and probably a good third of them had been demolished. They were afraid to return to their villages; they feared their Muslim neighbors who had stripped them of their property, violated their wives and daughters, and killed many of their relatives. A British officer wrote that the collapse of Russia in the civil war had allowed the Ottomans to advance deep into Persia, encircling Assyrian towns and villages in the Urmia region and pushing into Azerbaijan. Not long after, the governor-general of the Persian province confirmed the substance of Assyrian grievances, stating that the Kurds of Urmia "were about to massacre some Assyrians" and then "plundered the surrounding villages, massacred the peasants, and occupied all the shores of Lake Urmia." When Assyrian refugees from Persia arrived in Iraqi refugee camps, the administrator observed an infant mortality rate so high "that it would have been simply racial suicide if this high rate of child mortality were allowed to continue." Approximately 3,000 refugees perished within a matter of months due to diseases such as dysentery, smallpox, cholera, measles, typhoid, and fevers. Up to 65,000 Assyrians died while fleeing north or southwest from the Urmia and Salmas regions. The killings of Assyrians in 1915, in particular, but also in other years, bore a resemblance to those that occurred in Srebrenica eighty years later. During that criminal episode, the killing of 7,000-8,000 Bosnian Muslim men was declared a genocide because it could "potentially" eliminate the entire Muslim population in Srebrenica. In fact, the Srebrenica killings were likely less severe than those of the Assyrians because they were preceded by the exchange of many Bosnian Muslims for Serbian prisoners, and because women and children were intentionally spared death, with orders issued for their safe transport away from the front lines. Four-fifths of the population captured by the Bosnian Serbs survived. The International Criminal Tribunal for the Former Yugoslavia concluded that the chief Bosnian Serb commander convicted of complicity in genocide knew that Bosniak men were being killed and did not prevent his subordinates from doing so, demonstrating his "genocidal intent."" Therefore, the tribunal found that genocide had been committed in Srebrenica, a decision upheld on appeal in 2004. The International Court of Justice echoed this conclusion in 2007. In 2015, Turkish Foreign Minister Ahmet Davutoğlu attended the anniversary event of the genocide in Bosnia and Herzegovina, and the following year, the office of his successor Mevlüt Çavuşoğlu released a statement confirming Turkey's view that Srebrenica was a genocide. As early as 2012, the Ministry of Foreign Affairs "condemned any attempt to downplay or deny the genocide that occurred in Srebrenica." After the war, the Turkish government informed the League of Nations that the Assyrians "were compelled to leave the country" for having attacked the Turks at the suggestion of the Russians. Genocidal deportations continued until the mid-1920s, when the Kemalists conquered the Iraqi-Turkish border region. The Kemalists gathered the Assyrians and displayed them as commodities to willing buyers, who paid small sums to acquire Assyrian women and young people. The deportees were destitute, emaciated, and "infested with parasites." A 1922 report from Near East Relief to the United States Secretary of State stated that, like the Armenians, "the deported Assyrians are now in a condition worse than slavery," with children suffering from hunger and not even having clothes to cover themselves.

The Assyrians

The Assyrian identity was intricate due to political and religious factors predating the First World War. Prior to delving into the Assyrian genocide and its commemoration, it is imperative to situate the Assyrian people in geographical regions and history. The Assyrian people share a homeland divided among four states, primarily encompassing the Nineveh Plains region in Iraq, the Ḥakkārī and Tur Abdin regions of Turkey, the Urmia region of Iran, and the area near the Khabur River and the Syrian city of Aleppo. Historically, the Assyrians migrated among these regions, both for trade and to escape persecution or as a result of deportation.

Ancient inscriptions and documents have confirmed an ancient Assyrian presence, ranging from the region near Nineveh (Mesopotamia) to former Assyrian colonies in the northeast (Persia) and northwest (Anatolia). The ancient Assyrian religion was practiced in southeastern Anatolia and northern Iraq before the conversion of many Assyrians to Christianity, and in its vestigial form of spells and superstitions probably up to the present day. The ancient Assyrian religion was

103

practiced in southeastern Anatolia and northern Iraq. Before the conversion of many Assyrians to Christianity, in nearby Harran until almost a thousand years after the death of Jesus Christ, and in southeastern Anatolia, northern Iraq, eastern Syria, and the far south of Iraq and Iran until the twentieth century in the attenuated forms of Yazidism and Mandaeism. Christianity emerged alongside the ancient Assyrian religion, not after its disappearance. The ancient names and stories of the Assyrians also persist in the attenuated form of Yazidism, Mandaeism, and Magianism/Zoroastrianism in eastern Anatolia, Iran, Iraq, and Syria. Assyrian Christian populations descend from groups that practiced ancient Assyrian religions and lived in a place called Āṯūr (Assyria) when Christianity arrived.

According to the 6th-century AD Christian history of Assiria by Mshihā Zkhā, Addai was the apostle to "Adiabene and Assyria" and appointed Pqīdhā as bishop of that region. In Eastern Christian tradition, Saint Thomas the Apostle sent Addai to evangelize the East, where Assyrian and Babylonian doctrines of the fallen yet resurrected

Lord who became the King of Kings had long prevailed. Assyria and nearby Arbelā (Arbela/Irbil) had Christian bishops between 100 and approximately 250 years after the death of Jesus Christ. The Assyrian oral tradition is that the Assyrians settled in Urmia during the time of the ancient Assyrian empire. History states that the people of Edessa advised Saint Thomas to preach to the Assyrians of Urmia, with whom the Edessans were familiar. Within another century or so, there were over twenty bishops in the swath of territory from 'Ūrhāy (Edessa/Urfa/Ourfa) in Anatolia across Armenia and Assyria into Persia. By the early 5th century, under the Persian Empire, there were nearly forty-six bishoprics. Niniveh became the seat of a Christian bishop and a place where the Eastern Church and the Syriac Orthodox Church vied for popularity. As the Apostles might have expected, medieval and early modern Assyrian churches did not contain images, relics, or statues. The Assyrian church preserved precious manuscripts written in Aramaic, the language spoken by Jesus, until the Kurds entered its churches, which had been built with defense in mind using thick stones, and plundered or destroyed the texts and everything else. That the "Assyrians" survived as a people and not merely as inhabitants of a geographical area is evident from the description in ancient texts of the pagan heritage of the Edessan Christians, which included the worship of Assyrian gods Bel, Nabu, and Ningal, rather than Aramean gods Hadad, Atargatis, and Śahr/Śehr. Syriac martyrdom and early church chronicles also confirm the conversion of Edessan Christians from the worship of Assyrian gods Bel and Nabu. The early church in Mesopotamia contended with Assyrian magic before the 7th century AD. Ancient Assyrian rituals, such as the "medicine of life," were used in Syriac Orthodox liturgy. Akkadian terms for father and brother, bread and water, sun and moon, among others, are still in use in "Syriac." The acts of praise for the Assyrian gods appeared in reference to the Christian God, Christ, and the earthly church. The Assyrians continued to honor Šameš, the Sun God, even during the Christian era, in Adiabene (which extended from Erbil to Tur Abdin) and the rest of Persian Assyria. Even in the nineteenth century, the Assyrians persisted in casting ancient magical spells. The patriarch of the Edessan Christians, Michael Rabo, identified his flock as the "Oturoye," or the Assyrians of Mesopotamia. Bar Hebraeus, the Catholicos of the Syriac Orthodox Church and chronicler of his patriarchate, identified Assyria as a key region where his church was active. With the spread of Christianity, the Assyrians began to convert their temples into churches or destroy them and to forbid the ancient Assyrian rituals by adopting Judeo-Christian names. However, cities like Ḥarrānu or Κάρραι (Harran), Hatra [Ḥaṭrā], Beth Garma, and Nippur continued to serve as sites for ancient Assyrian rites and remnants of the Assyrian-Babylonian cult. Even in the Christian stronghold of Edessa, ancient Assyrian practices such as the use of magical spells, medicine, and divination persisted at least until the 5th century AD. In 1553, the Catholic Church established a Catholic patriarchate for the Assyrians, inviting a Nestorian Christian leader to assume this role. The Vatican established this patriarchate for "the Assyrian nation," or the Chaldeans. However, the Chaldeans [Keldânî or Kildani or Keldoye] retained many Assyrian customs. Assyrian communities continued to exist in the twentieth century. When they arrived in the United States, not only the "Eastern Assyrians" but also the Syriac Orthodox Christians, sometimes now referred to as "Arameans," actually identified themselves and their churches as "Assyrians." Furthermore, at the Paris Peace Conference, the Syriac Orthodox Patriarchate (of Antioch), under the signature of Mor Ignatius Severius Aphrem I Barsoum, called for the "emancipation" and compensation of the residents of Upper Mesopotamia, "our ancient Assyrian nation." Despite this history, the Assyrians have sometimes been known by various denominational and quasi-denominational terms such as "Nestorians," Chaldeans, Jacobites, Syrians, Syriacs, and "Syriac-speaking Christians." "Syrian" is the English form, "Syrien" is the French, and "Syrer" is the German rendition of the modern Assyrian or Neo-Aramaic term "Sūrāyā," or in Arabic or Turkish "Süryân," which becomes "Sūryāyē" or "Süryânî" when referring to the people. This is why, in Turkish, the Assyrian genocide is sometimes known as the

Syrian/Nestorian or "Süryanı Nasturi Soykirim." Some of these are incorrect because modern Assyrians, including Syriac Orthodox Christians often known as "Syrians" in the nineteenth and early twentieth centuries, do not speak literary Syriac. The International Association of Genocide Scholars has used "Assyrian" as a generic term for Nestorians, Chaldeans, Jacobites, Syrians, Arameans, and "Syriacs." Similarly, Adam Jones, an expert genocide scholar, argues that "Assyrian" is historically the prevailing term for the various indigenous inhabitants of northwestern Persia, southeastern Anatolia, and Upper Mesopotamia. Furthermore, religious historian Dorothea Weltecke and other scholars have demonstrated that the patriarchate of the medieval Syriac Orthodox Church, the Church of Antioch, described the ancient Assyrians as the ancestors of the Christians in the region. The identities of the Assyrians before 1915 may have been tied to local contexts rather than a national or transnational identity narrative. Literacy was limited, and nationalist literature began to be printed and distributed from the late 18th to the early 20th century. Activists like Surma d'Bait Mar Shimun,

Agha Petros, and Mor Severius Barsoum, each of whom attempted with a limited degree of success to establish a common Assyrian identity among religious denominations and differences in language or dialect among them. A prevalent unifying factor was the use of Neo-Aramaic language at home; although this was not universal, it might have been common among the ancestors or neighbors of the Assyrians. However, their elite understood that they lived in Assyria and expressed this in their correspondence with the Vatican, to Western travelers, and in internal chronicles and manuscripts. Syriac religious texts, along with earlier Jewish and Roman sources long predating British or French imperial contact, referred to the people as Assyrians. The use of Assyrian as a self-designation in premodern times, but after the fall of Assyria and the rise of Greece, Rome, and Persia, is evident from Herodotus, Persian inscriptions, church historians like Michael the Syrian, and correspondence between the Catholic Church and the Church of the East or the Chaldeans. While the Assyrians were divided by denomination into various Eastern Rite churches, they understood that they spoke the same language beyond these divisions. Eastern Rite churches, or "Syriac" ones distinct from the Armenians, Greeks, Copts, and Maronites, were sometimes referred to as Chaldeans, Church of the East or Nestorians, Syriac Orthodox or Jacobites, and Syriac Catholics. Hence, apart from the many references to the so-called "Syriac Christians" as Assyrians in premodern times, stating that Aramaic ["ārāmāye"] was the typical self-designation of the Suryaye before British influence in the region is inaccurate. Far from being a recent term, as scholars Butts, Joseph, Wilmshurst, and others suggest, "Aššūrāyu" (Assyrian) is an ancient self-designation, and its orthographic variant "Sūrāyu" (Syria) is the original version of the medieval and modern self-designations Sūrāyā and Sūryōyō. According to an ancient Luwian inscription dedicated to an Anatolian vassal or ally of ancient Assyria, "Assiro" was translated as "Syrian" [SHRYM and su+ra/i] in Phoenician and Luwian, cultures from which the Greeks might have learned. For these reasons, "Assyrian" is a convenient shorthand for populations with Aramaic language roots and Syriac reading traditions, or for adherents of

Syriac Rite churches (Chaldeans, Nestorians, and Protestants converted from Chaldean or Nestorian churches).

The advantages of "Assyrian" over Aramaic are twofold: (1) the stronger geographic association of Upper Mesopotamia and northwestern Persia with Assyria as opposed to the Aramean kingdoms, which were situated further west in present-day Syria; and (2) avoiding reference to the biblical myth of Aram, the son of Shem, although some Christians used it to designate Eastern Christians. There is little justification for distinguishing Āmid (Diyarbakir or Diarbekir/Diarbeck) and its surroundings from the Mosul region, as the Church of the East in the seventeenth century was divided into "Āmid of Assyria" and Babylon, Arbil, Hakkari, Basra, and Persia. However, some scholars disagree with the use of "Assyrian" as a generic term. Mark Levene, for instance, may have influenced other genocide scholars when he claimed that the very word "Assyrian" was a piece of orientalist propaganda. He has proposed that the identity commonly referred to by most historians and genocide scholars writing about the late Ottoman Empire as "Assyrian" is actually "a religious creed" called "Syrian." Levene correctly noted that his perspective is in line with that of John Joseph of Franklin & Marshall College. Joseph and Sebastian Brock have asserted that "Assyria" was a term coined by Europeans for the Aramaic-speaking people of Upper Mesopotamia. Joseph undermined his own position when, following criticism, he acknowledged that Herodotus referred to the people of Mesopotamia and the Mosul region as Assyrians in an ethnic or racial sense. He also admits that the Catholic, Anglican, and American churches referred to the Suraye/Suryaya as "Assyrians" prior to World War I.

Statistics on the Assyrian Population

According to British and Russian sources, in the first decade of the twentieth century, there were up to 863,000 Assyrians in Asian Turkey. Their population radiated to the south, east, and west from its center near the patriarchal seat of Mar Shimun in Qūdshānīs (Qudshanis or Kochanes) (in Turkish: Konak). Approximately 165,000-

190,000 Assyrians lived in the mountains before 1915. Consul Trotter, a representative of the British Empire in Eastern Anatolia, estimated that 259,600 Assyrians (Nestorians and other Eastern Christians) lived in the vilayets of Van (including Hakkari), Diyarbakir, Erzurum, and Harput [Kharpout] [Turkish: Ma'muretü'l'âziz]. The Syriac Orthodox Church had between 150,000 to 200,000 members. Alongside 100,000 Syriac Orthodox and Chaldean or Syriac Catholics in the province of Diyarbekir, there were estimates of 200,000 Syriac Orthodox throughout the entire Ottoman Empire before 1915. The Syriac Orthodox patriarch identified the affected areas as encompassing "the provinces of Bitlis, [Seert], and Kharpout, and their dependencies, in Mesopotamia; the provinces of Diarbekir, Mardin, and their dependencies, and Ourfa," which is to say, eastern Anatolia or eastern Turkey. The Ottoman Assyrian population would have exceeded half a million in 1914, judging by the rate of growth of comparable populations. Massacres and small-scale deportations are not necessarily incompatible with a certain population growth because impoverished and poorly

114

educated individuals with limited access to advanced medical services tend to have more children. A British vice-consul believed that as many as 500,000 Assyrians were residing in the Ottoman Empire in 1879. By the end of 1890, it seems reasonable to presume an Ottoman Assyrian population of 600,000, given a population growth of 25% over the twenty years from 1879 to 1899. Another possibility is that the diplomat may have overestimated, and that the Assyrian-Chaldean delegation at the Paris Peace Conference was closer to the exact number, referring to approximately 350,000 Assyrians in the province of Diyarbakir, Hakkari, or Seert/Siirt/Sa'irt/Saird, and the northern parts of the Urfa/Aleppo region, with the population having been reduced by the massacres of 1894–1896. There were approximately 140,000 Assyrians in Persia during the mid-nineteenth century. The sum of Ottoman and Persian Assyrian totals yields an overall Assyrian population of 740,000.

Assyrian History in the 19th Century

Nineteenth-Century British Travelers in the Middle East described the Assyrians as a "bold and resilient race" who fiercely defended their mountainous territories, properties, and churches "by force of arms." Their population covered the southeastern corner of what is now Turkey, the northwestern corner of what is now Iran, and the northwestern corner of what is now Iraq. From the Persian conquest to the partition of the Ottoman Empire, the northernmost Eastern Assyrians in Ottoman lands often submitted to the temporal and spiritual jurisdiction of the patriarch of the Church of the East, Mar Shimun. Its headquarters were in Qudshanis, north of Julamerk, west of Urmia, and northeast of Tur Abdin. In the mid-nineteenth century, the Islamic emir of Hakkari and the Kurdish warlord Bedr Khan Beg targeted and killed the Assyrians, including the patriarch's family. The Turkish governor of the Pashalic (the pasha's jurisdiction) of Mosul authorized Bedr Khan to "punish the Christians." According to one report: "Troops were dispatched in every direction to lay waste to the surrounding villages. The war had become little more than a series of massacres. The Kurds moved from place to place, killing the

116

people." The British diplomat Austen Henry Layard wrote, "In 1843, Bedr Khan Bey invaded the districts of Tiyari, cold-bloodedly massacring nearly ten thousand of their inhabitants and enslaving a great number of women and children." A substantial portion of the Assyrian population in Hakkari was exterminated. Thousands of Assyrians perished in the Ottoman massacres of 1895. An Assyrian religious scholar in Mosul, writing in 1895, recounted how Christian massacres unfolded in the city of Amid and the surrounding villages, as well as in Se'erd and Batlis; and in all the countryside and towns and villages where there were Syrians and Armenians, they were mercilessly killed. Their wives and children were taken away as prisoners. Anahit Khosroeva, a genocide historian, also writes that during this period, large-scale abductions of women occurred. The events actually began in 1894 when ten thousand Armenians were massacred, after which another 4,000 were killed in the Sivas region by Kurdish forces, and 800 were killed in the Harput area. The British Blue Book on Turkey mentioned 8,000 Armenians or other Christians killed in the

Diyarbakir region in 1895-1896, with over 500 Armenian girls and children abducted by Kurds there and in the Silvan area. Another British official tasked with investigating some of these events, along with two Ottoman officials, reported that 8,000 Armenians had perished in Edessa/Urfa, with Ottoman mobs proclaiming that "no Christian should be left in the country." British diplomats lodged complaints with the Ottoman Foreign Ministry in 1896 because over 100 "Christians remain in the hands of the Kurds," presumably having been abducted and expressing "fear." A French study remarked that in "Bitlis, Van, Harput, the same horrors occurred, naturally followed by extreme destitution."

Religion and Territorial Security in Late Ottoman History

From Humble Beginnings in the Early 14th Century, Ottoman Politics Marched Across Continents to Compete with European Empires and Persia for Dominance over Eurasia. While Most of Its History and Politics Extend Beyond the Scope of This Volume, It Is Necessary to Briefly Review the Form of Government, the Role of Religion, and the Geopolitical Situation of the Empire. The Ottoman Sultan Inherited Modes of Governance and Territorial Divisions from the Caliphs of Islam, the Eastern Roman Emperors, and the First Two Turkic-Islamic Empires, the Seljuks and the Timurids. Politically, the Sultan was an absolute ruler, leading to accusations of "Oriental despotism," especially from the English and Germans. In practice, however, the Sultan's power was divided and constrained by the systems of zimmi (protection; Arabic: dhimmī) and millet (religion or religious community; Arabic: milla); a quasi-nobility of viziers (administrative advisors), pashas (lords), aghas (leaders or commanders), and corporations; the Meclis-i Mebûsân or lower house of the parliamentary council known as the House of Deputies and the Meclis-i Ayan or upper house known as the House of Notables; the role of Western consular officials and financiers; and the poor state of communications and infrastructure. It is particularly likely that Turkmen and Kurdish tribes and tribal confederations enjoyed local autonomy, argue some scholars. The millet system allowed leaders of controlled religious minorities to adjudicate religious matters,

119

administer religious properties, and handle often minor issues. The lack of personal security and exclusion from significant political and administrative roles afflicted minority communities, particularly in the period preceding the "Capitulations" of 1839-1876, until a series of mass atrocities erupted during the Balkan and Armenian struggles, as well as during Kurdish and Circassian expansionist ambitions. European powers, especially Britain, France, and Russia, exerted pressure on the Ottomans to enhance the rights of Christian subjects and reform certain laws. The millet system appears to have begun as a more localized and almost democratic system for selecting city leaders, at least in urban areas, which evolved into a hierarchical mode of representation, where the religious leader of a community had access to the Sultan, and their local delegates could sit in provincial councils. By way of exemption from Sharia financial law, the system particularly assisted Armenians, Greeks, and Jews in succeeding in trade and finance. The Seljuks and later the Ottomans capitalized on the weakness of Assyria and Babylonia, Persia, Byzantium, and the Slavic nations due to climate changes, the Roman-Persian conflict, Arab conquests, and subsequently the Black Death and Turkic-Mongol migrations. The Ottoman Empire is believed to have expanded to a size larger than its Roman predecessor and maintained a higher level of economic activity than any Western state or empire of its era. The Ottomans reached the present-day border between Turkey or Iraq and Iran in the 16th century and were especially active in the 1400s and 1500s in slave raids across what is now Serbia, Albania, Bosnia, Hungary, Germany, Italy, Spain, Poland, the Caucasus, and Russia. Russian politics may have been permanently shaped by the legacy of Mongol and Ottoman incursions, which made the Crimean region home to hundreds of thousands of Slavic captives by the 1600s. Russian leaders viewed the fall of Byzantium to the Turks as a dire warning. Russia continued to assert a protective role over the Rûm or Greek Orthodox Christians of the Ottoman Empire, who typically used Greek script to correspond in the Ottoman Turkish dialect. This community included many Arabic speakers, as well as the Syriac Orthodox community, although in many cases, it is not clear what the original nation or ethnicity of these Arabic-speaking individuals was. The Rûm also encompassed speakers of Slavic languages, especially in Constantinople. However, the Rûm are generally referred to as Ottoman Greeks, even though many traditionally Greek areas also had Arab and Slavic Christian residents. French and Italian Roman Catholic missionary activity expanded into the empire in the seventeenth century, eventually claiming alliances with influential Armenian clerics, members of the Church of the East, Syriac Orthodox, and Greek Orthodox (e.g., in Aleppo and the areas between Mosul and Diyarbakir). Embracing a European faith offered the hope of securing European protection under the Capitulations and through the diplomatic efforts of consular officials. Literacy also improved, in part due to the efforts of missionary schools. The borders of European empires expanded into former Ottoman territories. France occupied Algeria (1830) and Egypt (1798), followed by Britain in Egypt and Sudan (1882); Austria entered Transylvania (1683), Hungary (1699), Serbia (1699–1718 and 1788–1792), Moldavia and Wallachia [Romania] (1789), and

Bosnia (1878); Russia attacked Ukraine (1674–1696), Moldavia and Wallachia (1769, 1806, and 1829), Transylvania (1849), Circassia (1863), Crimea (1783), Kabardia (1769–1774), and Ossetia (1774); and Italy conquered Libya (1911) and parts of the Horn of Africa (around 1885 and 1909–1911). Russia also occupied Bukhara (1868) and Khiva (1873); it took parts of Azerbaijan (1806–1809), Dagestan (1812), and Georgia (1800) from the Persian Empire; and nearly conquered Western Armenia and the Pontic Greece (now Eastern Turkey) controlled by the Ottomans in 1877–1878. Russia played a prominent role in supporting the independence of Greece (1830), Bulgaria (1878), and Serbia (1806–1812 and 1878). The British doctrine of the balance of power contributed to a relatively long period of peace in Europe, with dramatic exceptions such as the Franco-Prussian War and a range of conflicts in the Balkans and Black Sea region between 1815 and 1914. Jurist Emerich de Vattel referred to the doctrine as "an arrangement of affairs so that no State is capable of absolute mastery and dominion over the others." Thus, the War of Spanish Succession preserved the balance against a combination of French and Spanish forces and their satellites, while the Napoleonic Wars prevented the merger of France, Germany, Spain, and Russia into a continental empire; the Crimean War kept the Eastern Mediterranean, Black Sea shores, and the Caucasus out of Russian hands; the World Wars were fought to safeguard, among other things, France and Russia from Germany; and the Cold War aimed to break the Warsaw Pact connecting East Germany, the northern Balkans, Poland, the Baltic states, the Caucasus, and Russia. Great Britain allied with the Ottomans and Russia against France during the Napoleonic era and with the Ottomans against Russia in the mid-1800s. London also viewed the Ottomans and Persians as useful buffers between its empire and Russia. Perhaps Russia's primary objective leading up to World War I was Constantinople and the Turkish Straits, which would have allowed Russia to access the Mediterranean from the Black Sea and secure a port. Both Great Britain and France were against this possibility. With British training of their fleet and the construction of a battleship, the Ottomans were poised to achieve naval superiority over the

Russian Empire, which would have posed a serious threat to Russian exports. At the same time, Russia represented a threat to British interests in India and Persia. Britain failed to assist the Ottomans in their conflicts against the Italians in Libya or the Balkan League in 1912, effectively dismantling the "pro-Ottoman European coalition" from the 1850s. European and American influences overlapped in the areas inhabited by the Assyrians of the Ottoman Empire and Persia. In the 1840s and 1850s, British diplomacy played an "instrumental" role in pressuring the Ottomans to halt a campaign of extermination against the northwestern Assyrian communities. In 1869, the Church of the East complained to Russia that Kurdish tribes were "constantly kidnapping our virgins, brides, and women." During the war, the American Minister Plenipotentiary in Persia, John Caldwell, wrote to the Persian Empire's Minister of Foreign Affairs, inquiring whether, in light of the "massacre" of Assyrians in Diliman, the Persian government could ensure the safety of "American citizens and other Christians in Urmia." The French Lazarist order, the Church of England mission among the

Assyrians, and American Protestant organizations, including the American Board of Commissioners of Foreign Missions, established schools and published books for the Assyrians. The Russian Orthodox Church also drew followers, particularly from the Eastern Church. It has been written that one or more Kurdish leaders had a saying that the Assyrians were the "Little Russia" and that exterminating them would serve to defeat the "Great Russia."

The concept of genocide

The founder of the Genocide Convention, Raphael Lemkin, developed a framework for analyzing cases of genocide that is highly applicable to the study of the Assyrian tragedy. While his focus was on the Nazis and the "Axis government," Lemkin wrote about genocides during the persecution of Christian sects by the Roman Empire and the Holy Roman Empire, as well as during episodes more akin to the massacres of Ottoman Christians in the nineteenth century than the larger massacres in 1915. Lemkin likely viewed genocide as a form of intense persecution or forced assimilation. He defined the communist persecution of Christian clergy during his lifetime as a type of genocide and described them as genocidal policies "that interfere with the activities of the Church." In acknowledging a communist genocide in the 1950s, Lemkin emphasized that "genocide is a concept that carries the highest moral condemnation in our Cold War against the Soviet Union" and that "the resort to genocide [by communist governments] is threatening our civilization." While drafting his plan for an autobiography, Lemkin explained that the Convention had saved "five nations" between 1948 and 1955; he may have had in mind Ukraine, Hungary, and the Baltic states of Latvia, Lithuania, and Estonia. Lemkin's concept of "cultural genocide," as later articulated within the United Nations Human Rights Council, encompasses "[any] action aimed at or having the effect of depriving [peoples] of their integrity as distinct peoples, or of their cultural values or ethnic identities" or "[any] form of assimilation or integration by other cultures or lifestyles imposed through legislative, administrative, or other measures." During Lemkin's time, Germanization or Aryanization was a typical way to analyze the Nazi genocide of Jews, Poles, Slavs, and Roma. The text of the Genocide Convention and Lemkin's vision as its founder indicate the broad scope of the concept of genocide. Lemkin wrote: In general, genocide does not necessarily mean the immediate destruction of a nation unless it is accomplished by mass killings of all members of a nation. Genocide has two phases: one involves the destruction of the national pattern of the oppressed group, and the other entails the imposition of the oppressor's national pattern. Consequently, Article II of the Genocide Convention includes various forms of genocide that do not require killing and, in fact, may assume the survival of the affected victims: inflicting serious physical or mental harm on members of the group, interfering with births within a group, and forcibly transferring children from one group to another. Lemkin stated that the genocide crime should also encompass "the gradual and scientific homicide by mass starvation or the rapid but equally scientific mass extermination in gas chambers, executions, or exposure to diseases and exhaustion." Article II(c) of the Convention recognized that intentionally imposing living conditions designed to destroy a group, such as the absence of food or medical care, is also a form of genocide. An increase in infant mortality rates, which Lemkin deemed genocidal, could also trigger Article II(d) of the Convention, addressing interference with the reproductive process. Lemkin also asserted that genocide could target the economic, emotional, religious, artistic, or scientific life of a group: genocide is, as we have noted, a collection of various acts of persecution or destruction. Many of these acts, when they constitute a violation of honor and rights, when they infringe upon life, private property, and religion, or science and art, or even when they unduly encroach upon the realm of taxation and personal services, are prohibited by Articles 46, 48, 52, and 56 of the Hague Regulations. Lemkin witnessed genocide when "the necessities of life like warm clothing, blankets, and firewood in winter were withheld or requisitioned from Poles and Jews." In his view, separating family members for deportation, conquest, or enslavement was a genocide:

"Millions of prisoners of war and forced laborers from all conquered countries in Europe were kept away from contact with their wives." Poles in incorporated Poland encountered obstacles when trying to marry among themselves. The removal of children and their Germanization in German schools was part of the genocide, according to Lemkin: "The Germans sought to erase all traces of previous cultural patterns. Attendance at a compulsory German school through elementary grades and three years of secondary school. Preventing genocide required criminal accountability based on the "formulation and teaching of the criminal philosophy of genocide" and the "tolerance" of genocide by governments or political parties, as well as the actual genocidal acts. Therefore, the Convention prohibits both "incitement to commit" and "complicity in genocide." As the "founder" of the Genocide Convention, Raphael Lemkin also inferred the intent of genocide from the factors used by the courts. He spoke of genocides during the persecution of Christian sects by the Roman Empire and the Holy Roman Empire, as well as during episodes more akin to what happened in

Ṭiyārī (Tiyari) in the 1840s or in Adana in 1909 than in Diyarbakir in 1915. Writing about Native Americans, Lemkin emphasized enslavement and deprivation of homes and economic necessities as genocides. When discussing the communist genocide in the 1950s, Lemkin emphasized that victims were deported, spiritual leaders were targeted, and not only that, but massacres also occurred. Most of the genocides identified by Professor Lemkin throughout human history have been instances of religious violence on a horrifying scale. While he undoubtedly saw and recognized signs of anti-Semitic persecution all around him as a person of Jewish descent, he was initially troubled by the massacres of Armenians by the Turks. During the last decade of his life, Lemkin focused on the suffering of Christians during communism in Eastern Europe and formed a coalition to use the concept of genocide to condemn such crimes, even though, by his estimation, they occurred on a much smaller scale than the events of 1914-1926. Courts and parliaments echoed his findings after the fall of the Berlin Wall. International criminal tribunals adopted the broader interpretation of genocidal intent that extends to cultural and religious devastation, not just racial extermination. Both the International Criminal Tribunal for the former Yugoslavia and the United Nations have concluded that "the destruction of historical, religious, or cultural heritage does not in itself qualify as genocide but may be considered as evidence of the intent to physically destroy a group." In the first decision of the International Criminal Tribunal authorized by the Security Council under the Genocide Convention, the International Criminal Tribunal for Rwanda established that the "systematic eviction from homes" by the Rwandan government of the Tutsi ethnicity was a form of genocide under Article II(c). In the first genocide conviction to emerge from the United Nations-backed Yugoslav tribunal, the court held that, although it was "impossible to determine with precision the number of Bosnian Muslim men killed by Serb-Bosnian forces," a military officer had become an accomplice to genocide by aiding subordinates who had "the intent to eradicate a group within a limited geographical area such as a country's region or even a municipality."

The same tribunal also ruled that forcibly expelling a group from the country or local area while burning their homes could constitute genocide because it prevents the group's return. National courts have also convicted defendants for smaller massacres, including those perpetrated by the Ethiopian communist regime against its opponents in the 1980s, and by Iraq against Kurdish communities situated near the frontlines of the Iran-Iraq War and the Kurdish uprising.

Assyrian Transmission of Ottoman Christian Genocide Testimonies

Immediately after the massacres of 1915, reports were published by non-Assyrians. For instance, the Los Angeles Times ran the story of an Assyrian from Urmia who confirmed the extermination of the city's Christians, the destruction of surrounding villages, and the death of 200,000 innocents while survivors battled starvation. William Walter Rockwell, a member of the American Committee for Armenian and Syrian Relief, published a report in 1916 indicating that during World War I, "a large number" of Assyrians had perished due to massacres in the highlands north of Mosul and as a result of Turkish occupation of Persia. Subsequently, he published a book containing the account of Abraham Shlemon, who wrote that Kurdish tribes from the Jezireh region along the Persian border were plotting to exterminate the Assyrians to prevent a Russian invasion of the area. Rockwell also included the narrative of Paul Shimmon, in which he recounted how the remaining Assyrians fled to the Persian-Russian border, where many perished due to starvation, exposure to cold, privation, and diseases. In February 1916, the British government tasked James Bryce and Arnold Toynbee with compiling a report on the events in Armenia. Among the evidence compiled by Bryce and Toynbee were testimonies from Assyrians documenting the destruction of forty villages near Berwar and 8,500 deaths in a short period in the vicinity of Urmia. Foreign diplomatic documents often read as dry lists of cities and populations that were destroyed or subjected to atrocities. The fresher sense of Assyrian memory of the Ottoman Christian genocide is conveyed through books written in the late '10s and early '20s by authors like Joseph (Jean) Naayem, Yonan Shahbaz, and Abraham Yohannan, Assyrians who wished to communicate to a broader audience what was happening to their communities. In 1916, Yohannan, a professor at Columbia University in New York, wrote that Turkish and Kurdish forces had massacred many of the Assyrian men in Hakkari, with a total number of approximately 30,000 individuals, mostly women and children, who were heading as refugees towards northern Persia, where the survivors were often "hungry and homeless." He contended that complete massacres had occurred in communities like Hassan, Jezireh, Mansuriyeh, Sheikh, and Seert. He wrote that due to their likely small numbers and lack of representation, [the Assyrians] had garnered almost no interest. They had no advocates in the cities of Europe and Asia. In the highlands of Turkey and Persia, they have no leader or counselor and are rarely visited by travelers. [However,] the tragedy inflicted upon

135

the Syrian Nestorians in Urumia, Persia, in proportion to their number and social status, is scarcely matched and never surpassed in history. Yohannan concluded that Turkish and Persian forces had joined together to wage a "holy war" against the Christians. Meanwhile, Shahbaz described a personal ordeal; he had fled with his wife from hundreds of armed men intent on killing, witnessing orphans and children left on the road and thousands of Assyrians dying of hunger or during their flight from Persia. In 1921, Joseph (Jean) Naayem, an Assyrian who had served as a chaplain for Allied prisoners in Turkey, published his memoirs. His father had been killed in prison, reassured of his family's safety but later accused of aiding rebels. Claiming at the outset to be an "eyewitness and victim" of the "atrocities and massacres perpetrated by the Turks," the book reproduces "detailed narratives provided [to him] personally by eyewitnesses or true survivors of the persecution, who had miraculously endured their sufferings." The book also contains Naayem's firsthand account of the massacre of 5,000 Christians in the city of Urfa by Ottoman forces when he was seven years old.

Other Assyrians attempted to convey what was happening to their communities. The Chaldean archbishop[21] of Diyarbakir penned a letter published in The Times of London, asserting that all young Chaldeans compelled into Ottoman service had perished, followed by a massacre of the remaining males, a famine among widows and orphans, and the devastation of homes, churches, and schools.

Foreign Confirmation of Assyrian Genocide Narratives

A British dossier on Turkish war criminals recounted how Turkish gendarmes entered Assyrian villages and incited Kurdish bands to massacre the population, as at least one gendarmerie commander enslaved Armenian girls and enriched himself through plunder. Similarly, a British administrator in the former Ottoman province of Mosul described how Kurds captured

---

[21] The Chaldean Catholic Church is a patriarchal sui iuris Catholic church with communities in the Middle East, Europe, Oceania, and North America.

Assyrian women, led a large number of people to their deaths in inhospitable terrain, and looted Assyrian homes and religious buildings. A former Ottoman official described how Kurds and Ottoman forces massacred Assyrians and Armenians in the far eastern Anatolia from Diza to Mush, a stretch of towns and villages spanning about 200 miles. According to Sir Percy Cox[22], Assyrians in northwestern Persia had "virtually ceased to exist as a community." William Francis Hare, later British Minister of State for Colonial Affairs, noted that, despite attempting to aid the Allies in the war, the Assyrians were "surrounded by the Turks and short on ammunition, lost approximately two-thirds of their total number by the end of the war." Other senior officials claimed that the Assyrians had lost between one-third and half of their total number, possibly depending on whether the reference was to the overall Assyrian population or only the Turkish one. The British also denounced the Kemalists in 1925 for deporting the remaining Assyrian-Chaldean communities in southeastern Turkey; these

---

[22] Percy Zachariah Cox (Harwood Hall, November 20, 1864 – Melchbourne, February 20, 1937) was a British general and civil servant.

138

measures left the deported Christians in dire straits and led to the massacre of men and the deaths of hundreds more due to cold and famine. In 1919, Johannes Lepsius, a German Protestant missionary, published the significant collection of German archival material upon which many studies of the Armenian Genocide are based, even though scholars writing typically in the period 1919-1999 often omit to mention that the Assyrians are also mentioned in Lepsius' documents. These documents referred to deportations and/or massacres in many cities and towns: Amadia, Bashkala, Fayshkhabour, Jezireh, Mardin, Midyat, Nisibin, Tell Ermen, and elsewhere in northern Persia and the Ottoman provinces of Diyarbakir and Van. In June 1915, Ambassador Ernst Wilhelm Hohenlohe acknowledged in writing that the "Ottoman government is determined to eliminate the indigenous Christians." Lepsius' documents described how not only Turkish officials, mullahs, and civilians but also the British and French press and "public opinion in neutral countries" saw Germany as responsible for the crimes committed in Turkey due to its influence or even instigation of the Young Turks. They recognized that "all Christians, regardless of their ethnicity, suffered the same fate." A German Empire vice-consul wrote, "Germany's agreement with this mass murder of all Christians is presumed." The German ambassador noted that "among the Turkish population" in central Anatolia, "many believe" that the German government "was the instigator" of the Armenian genocide. As the "leading power in the alliance'" of the Central Powers, Germany must have been behind these "atrocities," as the British and French press (and perhaps the Russian as well) observed. A German officer in Anatolia, Field Marshal Colmar von der Goltz, received and approved the plan for the deportation and resettlement of populations. As a general, von der Goltz penned an article on the weakness of the Ottoman Empire, arguing that Islamization and the weakening of the Christian minority would be the solution to its problems. In November 1915, he ordered the Fourth Army to wage war against the Christians defending Midyat, who had been "besieged" and faced the threat of "massacres." A petition to the German Chancellor in October 1915 lamented that

Germany's "conscience" and "honor" were offended by the fact that "Innocent Christian blood is being shed in torrents at the hands of Muslims, and tens of thousands of Christians are being forced to convert to Islam," while Turkey enjoyed an alliance not only with Germany but with "all countries" in the spirit of "Islamic solidarity." The "Muslim population" viewed Germany's instigation or agreement "in part with approval," wrote a German vice-consul. After the nature of the deportations as a pretext for massacre was clarified to him, Ambassador Hans von Wangenheim in Constantinople wrote in defense of the Ottoman policy, characterizing it as an effort to "resettle in Mesopotamia" families from rebellious regions. German propaganda promoted endorsements of Ottoman policies that were triggering anti-Christian massacres. A report to Chancellor Bethmann Hollweg in 1917 described the Ottoman "strategy" of "inland resettlement without taking measures for their survival, exposing them to death, hunger, and disease." Similarly, in 1918, Henry Morgenthau, the American ambassador to the Ottoman Empire, delivered a significant speech condemning proposals to confine Armenians, Assyrians, and Greeks to submission under a nation-state dominated by Turkey after the war. He emphasized that Ottoman Turkish leaders and their allies had "completely massacred 2,000,000 men, women, and children: Greeks, Assyrians, Armenians; a staggering 1,500,000 Armenians." Ottoman Interior Minister Talât Pasha told him that the plan was not to leave the Christian populations in the country, as they could potentially rebel, as the Bulgarians had done, in collusion with Russia; their "passion for Turkifying the nation logically seemed to require the extermination of all Christians." Like reports to the German leadership, Morgenthau's memoirs asserted that Greek girls, just like Armenian girls, had been abducted and taken into Turkish harems, and Greek boys had been kidnapped and placed in Muslim households. Wherever the Greeks were gathered into groups and, under the so-called protection of Turkish gendarmes, were transported, mostly on foot, into the interior. He added that after the civilized world had not [sufficiently] protested against these deportations, the Turks later decided to apply the same methods on a larger scale not only to the Greeks but also to the Nestorians and other of his subjects. The notion that the Ottoman policy of genocide was directed against Armenians, rather than Christians in general, was challenged once more when the Vatican granted historian Michael Hesemann access to hundreds of previously unstudied pages in the Vatican Secret Archives. Hesemann announced to the Catholic news agency Zenit that the documents confirmed that there was a "UN-defined genocide and, simultaneously, the largest persecution of Christians in history, resulting in the deaths of 2.5 million people - 1.5 million Armenians and approximately one million Syrian and Greek Christians." He noted that Armenian women and children could be spared if they became slaves to Kurds or Turks, so these victims should be added to the tally. It is important to emphasize that Hesemann asserts, "Armenians were not killed because they were Armenians, but because they were Christians."

The decline in the Assyrian population illustrates the extent of the attacks on Assyrians. The Assyrian population in Anatolia plummeted from about 3-4% of the total population in 1880 to less than 0.5% in 1927. The 4% figure results from dividing the British estimate of 500,000 Assyrians in 1880 by the Ottoman census estimate of 11.85 million people in present-day Turkey in 1880. The Ottoman census estimate of 11.85 million people is the sum of provincial figures A figure below 3% results from dividing the British estimate of 500,000 Assyrians in 1880 by the French estimate for the sum of Armenian and Muslim populations in present-day Turkey in the 1890s. By dividing the estimated 71,000 Assyrians and Greeks in Turkey according to the 1927 census by the figure of 13.6 million people in Turkey at that time, you get a figure of approximately 0.5% of the Assyrian or Greek population in 1927. The Assyrian population in Persia declined from 2% in 1850 to 0.1% in 1956, with the Ottoman invasion in between. Few other genocides have left such a small residue. The overall Assyrian population is, therefore, many millions below the level it would have been if the cities and tribes of Assyria had not been decimated and scattered in the nineteenth and twentieth centuries. For instance, if there had been 500,000 Assyrians and one million Kurds in

144

the Ottoman Empire by the end of the nineteenth century, and if the Assyrian population had grown by a similar rate to that of the Kurdish population until 1990, there would have been six to seven million Assyrians in Turkey alone by 1990. Turkish Assyrians would have constituted a population similar in size to that of Azerbaijan in 1990 or Libya in 2011. In the aftermath of World War II, the Assyrian population faced the risk of complete oblivion. International diplomacy subordinated Assyrian survival to oil agreements, shifting military alliances, and ethnonationalism. The Assyrians were largely overlooked by the United Nations. Raphael Lemkin prepared several documents that analyzed these massacres as a genocide to be reckoned with alongside the Armenian genocide. However, unlike the Roma, these references to the Assyrians were not incorporated into the official United Nations reports dealing with genocide and its history. Even the founders of Israel regarded the Assyrians as a lesson from history. Yet, these facts remained forgotten for many years.

International Recognition of the Assyrian Genocide

In 2000, writer and activist Thea Halo documented and wrote about the Assyrian genocide. Her book, titled "Not Even My Name," belatedly drew attention to the Assyrian and Greek genocides alongside the more widely recognized Armenian genocide. Halo likely contributed to the adoption of a resolution recognizing the Armenian, Assyrian, and Greek genocides by the State of New York in the year 2000, which was reaffirmed in subsequent years. States other than New York have also recognized the Greek genocide, including Florida, Illinois, Massachusetts, New Jersey, Pennsylvania, and South Carolina. In 2006, Halo criticized the editors of a French parliamentary resolution on the denial of the Armenian genocide for entirely excluding Assyrian and Greek victims. Since 2006, recognition of the Assyrian genocide has occurred at an accelerated pace, as scholars' resistance has waned. In that year, the European Parliament recognized the Assyrian genocide. The European rapporteur on Turkey's progress towards EU accession also denounced Article 301 of the Turkish Penal Code, which prohibits criticism of race, the government, or the Turkish military because it hinders research on the Ottoman genocides. The European Parliament "emphasizes that, although recognition of the Armenian genocide is essential for a country on the path to accession to come to terms with and acknowledge its past," and that a similar need exists in the cases of the Assyrian and Greek genocides, so that Turkey "facilitates the work of researchers, intellectuals, and academics working on this issue, ensuring their access to historical archives and all relevant documents." In 2006, Hon. Stephen Pound presented a motion in the British Parliament for the recognition of the Assyrian genocide. In 2007, the International Association of Genocide Scholars issued a resolution acknowledging the Assyrian genocide. The International Association of Genocide Scholars issued a resolution in 2007 recognizing the Assyrian genocide. Three years later, the Swedish parliament passed a resolution urging the Swedish government to pressure Turkey to recognize the Assyrian and Greek genocides in the Ottoman Empire, along with the Armenian genocide. The resolution applied the definition of the Genocide Convention and stated that hundreds of thousands of Assyrians had fallen victim. In 2007 and 2010, the United States Congress considered resolutions to recognize and commemorate the Armenian genocide but withdrew them due to the Turkish threat to close U.S. bases in Turkey and supply lines in Iraq, and possibly elsewhere. Renowned historian Bernard Lewis, whose work played a pivotal role in persuading prominent American politicians to support the invasion of Iraq, asserted that "what happened to the Armenians was the result of a massive armed rebellion." By the end of October 2007, the sponsor of the recognition bill agreed to withdraw it, citing the potential Turkish invasion of northern Iraq. Another factor that may have influenced Congress's decision is that Turkey had blocked Armenia's overland routes to the west, citing the genocide recognition campaign as one of the primary reasons for doing so. The Bush administration opposed the resolution. Several former Secretaries of State wrote to the Speaker of the House, stating that "Turkey is an indispensable partner in our efforts in Iraq and Afghanistan, assisting the U.S. military in accessing Turkish airspace, military bases, and the border crossing with Iraq," and aiding U.S. interventions with its "NATO allies in the Balkans." In 2007, then-candidate Barack Obama condemned the "denial" of the Armenian genocide, and campaign official Samantha Power praised his ability to "speak truth to power" on this issue. However, after taking office in 2009, he ceased to speak truth to power about Turkey. On March 17, 2009, Congressman Schiff and seventy-six cosponsors introduced a resolution for the United States to "affirm" the Armenian genocide. The resolution's report documented that President Ronald Reagan had used the term "genocide" in 1981, while Presidents William J. Clinton and George W. Bush had referred to killings and massacres. On March 16, 2010, an aide to President Obama announced the administration's opposition to the resolution, suggesting that "our interest lies in a full, frank, and just recognition of the facts surrounding the events of 1915" by "the Armenian and Turkish peoples themselves." This was contrary to

Obama's approach to the Holocaust, Bosnia, Libya, Rwanda, Sudan, and Palestine, where he personally condemned genocide or human rights violations, rather than deferring to the peoples themselves to handle it in their own way. In 2012, instead of waiting for reports from joint commissions of Khmer Rouge supporters and their opponents, Hutu extremists and their opponents, Serbian-Bosnian nationalists and their opponents, or the Sudanese government and its opponents, President Obama likened the Holocaust to the killings in Cambodia, the killings in Rwanda, the killings in Bosnia, the killings in Darfur, which "shock our conscience." He likened this "madness" that permeates an entire nation to how "the Holocaust may have reached its barbaric peak at Treblinka, Auschwitz, and Belzec, but it began in the hearts of ordinary men and women." In 2009, President Obama noted that "the Holocaust was driven by many of the same forces that fueled atrocities" elsewhere and likened those who saved Jews from the Nazis to his commitment as president to prevent atrocities like those in Rwanda and Darfur, historical events that occurred before he took office. Also in 2009, he

150

stated, "The situation for the Palestinian people is intolerable. And America will not turn its back on the legitimate Palestinian aspiration for dignity, opportunity, and a state of their own." The situation of Turkish Christians, survivors of the genocide enduring the agony of their civilization, was tolerable. In 2011, he likened the situation in Libya to people being brutalized in Bosnia in the '90s as an example of "preventing genocide." Ten days earlier, he called for "international responsibility" for such killings of civilians. The United States' new policy of deference towards the successors of the perpetrators of these crimes also contrasted with the practice of Hillary Clinton, who repeatedly spoke of "genocide" in Bosnia, Cambodia, Iraq, Kosovo, Sudan, and Rwanda. Secretary Clinton declared these genocides without waiting for a commission's report or the blessing of the Sudanese people, for instance, even though she announced in 2010 that she and "her administration would work very hard to ensure that [the resolution on the Armenian genocide] never reached the floor of the House." Secretary Clinton likened a series of genocides to the Holocaust in 2012, asserting that 'what we mean when we say never again' is that 'at the end of the twentieth century, we witnessed campaigns of harassment and violence' based on race or religion, and "some that aimed at the destruction of a particular group of people, meeting the definition of genocide," including individuals who were "dragged from their homes" and "ethnically cleansed" in Kosovo, the 'massacre in the city of Benghazi,' and 'the ongoing violence in Syria." Representative Ileana Ros-Lehtinen of Florida, who became the chair of the House Foreign Affairs Committee in 2011, proposed that the resolution be rejected but that "any archive containing potentially relevant documents concerning the atrocities, warfare, and interethnic violence in the Ottoman Empire during that period, which has not been fully opened, should be immediately made available to both countries, a joint historical commission," and researchers. This was contrary to her practice in Bosnia, Cuba, Iran, Iraq, Libya, Saudi Arabia, Syria, and Venezuela, which involved her personally condemning past genocides and human rights violations rather than deferring to a joint commission of individuals supporting the alleged

152

perpetrators of genocide or other crimes and those opposing such mass atrocities. In 2010, the House Foreign Affairs Committee adopted Resolution 252 to recognize the Armenian genocide using the United Nations definition. The measure died after the full House declined to schedule a vote on it. In the United States, it is unlikely that the Assyrian genocide will be recognized at the federal level because, as once stated by Senate Majority Leader Bob Dole, "the only genocides we can talk about [in Congress] are those that do not embarrass an ally and do not threaten the profit margin of an American company." Therefore, the recognition of the Armenian genocide has been left to the White House rather than Congress, and presidents since George H.W. Bush have refrained from even mentioning Armenians as a case of genocide. Since 2010, individual states in the United States, as well as foreign nations, have shown increased activity in this field. In that year, California acknowledged the role of the Armenian and Assyrian massacres in inspiring Raphael Lemkin to coin the term "genocide" and designated April of each year as Genocide Awareness Month. In 2012-2013, the parliament of New South Wales, Australia, recognized the Armenian/Assyrian/Greek genocide. In 2013, several members of the Australian parliament endorsed a motion to recognize and condemn the Armenian genocide. Turkish diplomats have branded the resolutions as "incitement to hatred" against the Turkish race. In support of the New South Wales resolution, it was argued that Raphael Lemkin viewed the crime predominantly manifesting throughout history as an issue of cultural and religious nature. In 2014, the State of California mentioned Assyrians (and Syriacs), Pontians, and other Greeks in the context of the systematic killing of millions of people during the Armenian genocide. In 2014-2015, the Armenian and Greek parliaments recognized the Assyrian and Greek genocides, with the Greek parliament actually criminalizing the denial of the Assyrian and Greek genocides. The Vice President of the Armenian National Assembly explained, "We want to demonstrate to society, our Greek and Assyrian brothers and sisters, and the international community that the National Assembly of the Republic of Armenia and all political forces attach importance to condemning the genocide perpetrated against Greeks and Assyrians." The Russian Duma and the lower house of the Dutch parliament made similar moves in 2015. The German parliament recognized the Assyrians as victims in the adoption of a resolution commemorating the Armenian genocide in 2016. Therefore, there is now a consolidated academic and parliamentary record of Assyrian genocide recognition, with the possibility that its denial may be criminalized, as in Greece. Although the European Court of Human Rights ruled that people living in Europe have freedom of expression to deny the Armenian genocide, the Council of Europe has urged its members to enact laws criminalizing rhetoric that celebrates the Holocaust or the Armenian genocide in the context of xenophobia or hate speech. European law requires European Union member states to enact legislation to criminalize acts that condone, trivialize, or deny past genocides, crimes against humanity, or war crimes.

The Assyrians continue to suffer

The first recorded Assyrian genocide in modern times

The first recorded Assyrian genocide in modern times took place in 1843 in Hakkari (in present-day Turkey) at the hands of Kurdish forces under the command of Bedir Khan Beg. The genocidal campaign was orchestrated by Ottoman Turkish officials to quell the perceived threat of Assyrian independence: in the eyes of the Kurds, the presence of Assyrian tribes in the midst of their own settlements posed a significant challenge to their dominance in the region. At least ten thousand Assyrians were killed in the brutal massacres. Women and children were enslaved, and villages were plundered and set ablaze in the mountains where the Assyrians had lived nearly autonomously for thousands of years. Churches, villages, farmlands, and irrigation channels were utterly destroyed. The Assyrians mounted resistance to the attacks, but eventually, the Turkish army joined forces with Bedir Khan Beg and his troops. The various Assyrian tribes in the region were besieged, with no possibility of escaping the imminent massacres. According to an American missionary, "The Kurds swept through the region with fire and sword, sparing neither young nor old, male nor female, except for a few thousand they could carry away, destined for a fate worse than death." A brave group attempted in vain to confront the invaders but was quickly overwhelmed by superior numbers of enemies, and only four out of the forty heroes managed to escape. The entire Tyary, except for four or five villages, lay in ruins, the houses reduced to ashes. Some of the most revered churches, which had been sanctuaries for these people for centuries, were defiled and blasted into fragments with gunpowder. The precious library of the Patriarch was set ablaze, and amid the flames perished a collection of manuscripts beloved by the Assyrians and revered by all. According to eyewitness accounts: Assyrian children were tossed into the air and impaled with bayonets, many were burned alive, and some women threw themselves into a river with their small children bound to their backs to escape enslavement.

At the time, the Patriarch of the Church of the East was recognized as both the temporal and civil leader of the Assyrian people. Members of his family were murdered in the massacres, including his mother: the fate of the eighty-seven-year-old mother of the patriarch was horrible. Her aggressor assaulted her, and her body was then dismembered and set adrift on a raft, floating along the Zab River, where it was intercepted in the village of Chamba, the heart of the Tiyari district, with a note that read, "Your son will meet the same fate." Survivors of the attack were compelled to bear heavy loads of plunder as they journeyed on foot for extremely long distances. They were whipped and tortured along the way, and many were killed or perished from exhaustion. Bedir Khan Beg and the Kurdish allied forces conducted similar assaults on Assyrian villages in neighboring regions throughout 1840.

The Turkish Ottoman Genocide of the Assyrians

The Assyrian genocide began in the late 1914 and continued for over a decade, with the peak of violence occurring between 1915 and 1918. During these years, the Ottoman Turks (later the Republic of Turkey) and allied Kurdish tribes subjected hundreds of thousands of Assyrians to a systematic campaign of massacres, torture, abductions, deportations, impoverishment, and cultural and ethnic destruction. The campaign also

159

involved the destruction of historic Assyrian villages and cultural heritage sites, as well as the assassination of Assyrian intellectual and religious leaders. The massacres occurred in various phases across a wide area under Ottoman Turkish rule, including present-day Turkey, Iran, and Iraq. It is estimated that at least 300,000 Assyrians were killed during the genocide, and a large number were forced into permanent exile. Tragically, this figure represented at the time more than half of the entire Assyrian population. The aim of the Young Turks regime was to homogenize the Ottoman Empire by Turkifying the country and eliminating non-Turkish and non-Muslim communities. Ottoman and Turkish officials at the highest levels admitted policies that encouraged massacres, deportations, and deprivation of food and shelter. The Ottoman Turks and their Kurdish allies massacred hundreds of thousands of Assyrians, exterminated the Christian population, raped and enslaved hundreds or more likely thousands of Assyrian women in a systematic manner, and deported the population en masse from their ancestral lands under conditions that led to widespread famine and death. The policy of ethnic cleansing was promoted by stoking religious fanaticism. In 1914, the Ottoman Sultan declared a jihad (holy war) against "the enemies of Islam, who had demonstrated their hostility toward the Caliphate." It was these jihad declarations that facilitated the genocidal campaign against Christian communities in the Ottoman Empire, including Armenians, Greeks, and Assyrians, as they were considered infidels (kafir). There are numerous eyewitness accounts of the Assyrian genocide. In his book "Les Assyro-Chaldéens et les Arméniens massacrés par les Turcs," published in 1920, the Assyrian Father Joseph Naayem recounted, "I am determined to record the martyrdom of a small people, the most deserving of interest yet at the same time the most forsaken, born from a great empire and among the oldest civilizations, whose land, like Armenia, became a stage for Turkish abominations in which men were tragically murdered, women, children, and elders deported into the desert, plundered, tortured, and subjected to the worst atrocities." This people is the Assyrian-Chaldean people. How can I not provide the details of the tragic martyrdom of the Assyrians in the Jezireh district,

161

along the Tigris, and in Midyat, where over fifty villages, most of which I know by name, prosperous and fertile villages that would soon lie along the route of the great Baghdad railway line, promising a bright future, were utterly plundered and razed, while the majority of their population was put to the sword. Those who survived the massacres were forced into exile—what a heart-wrenching sight it was! A throng of 200,000 people, men, women, children, all on foot, going who knows where; all one could see along the road were wretched souls with swollen legs, pitiful elderly barely able to carry their load, small children crying, and grieving mothers weeping for their dead or lost children. Then, every so often, the Kurds would set upon those who were slower and massacre them. Finally, after a painful ten-day journey, this wretched population arrived in Russia, where many of them perished from hunger and disease." As for the city of Van, it was nearly entirely razed to the ground and destroyed. Many of those Assyrians fleeing from the genocide found refuge in certain parts of present-day Iraq, Syria, and Lebanon. The Reverend John Eshoo, who survived the horrific massacre in

Khoi (in present-day Iran), wrote: "You have undoubtedly heard of the Christian massacre in Khoi, but I am certain you are not acquainted with the details." Here is where a portion of our people had emigrated, and one-quarter of our refugees were stationed in Sardavar (Khoi). These Assyrians were gathered in a caravanserai and all shot to death. Blood literally flowed in small rivulets, and the entire open space within the caravanserai turned into a pool of crimson liquid. The place was too small to contain all the living victims for the execution operation. They were brought in groups, and each new group was forced to stand over the pile of still bleeding bodies and was shot with firearms in the same manner. The horrifying place literally became a human slaughterhouse, receiving its silent victims, in groups of ten and twenty at a time, for execution. The defenseless Assyrians marched like lambs to their slaughter, and they did not utter a word except to say, "Lord, into your hands we commend our souls." When the procession reached the designated location, the executioners began by cutting off their victims' fingers until both hands were completely amputated. Then they

163

were laid on the ground, in the manner of animals slaughtered in the East, but with their faces upturned and their heads resting on stones or blocks of wood. Their throats were then cut halfway through, prolonging their torment. And while they struggled in the throes of death, the victims were kicked and beaten by the heavy clubs wielded by the assailants. Many of them, still fighting for their lives, were thrown into ditches and buried before their souls had departed. The young and able-bodied were separated from the children and the elderly. They were taken a certain distance from the city and used as targets by snipers. They all fell, some not fatally wounded. One of the leaders approached the heap of the wounded and shouted loudly, swearing by the names of the prophets of Islam that those who had not received mortal wounds could get up and leave, as they would not be harmed any further. Some, thus deceived, rose, but only to fall dead this time under another hail of bullets from the assassins' rifles. Some of the younger and attractive women, along with some innocent-looking girls who begged to be killed, against their will, were forcibly taken into Islamic harems. Others were subjected to such diabolical insults that I cannot possibly describe. Death, however, came to their rescue and saved them from the vile passions of demons. The Assyrian victims of this massacre were countless. In March 1918, the Assyrian Patriarch Mar Shimun XXI Benyamin, who at the time was recognized as the religious and civic leader of the Assyrian people, was treacherously assassinated along with 150 others by the Kurdish chieftain Simko Shikak in Kuhnashahir, near Salmas during a ceasefire. While the scale of violence decreased, massacres against the Assyrians continued until 1925. The Assyrian genocide effectively decimated the Assyrian community and had a lasting impact. To this day, the Turkish government continues to deny the 1915 genocide. In 2007, the International Association of Genocide Scholars reached a consensus that the atrocities committed by the Ottoman Empire and later by the Republic of Turkey constituted a genocide against Armenians, Assyrians, and Greeks.

The Assyrian Massacre at Simele

The Simele Massacre, known to Assyrians as Pramta d'Simele, was a massacre committed by the armed forces of the Iraqi state, systematically targeting the indigenous Assyrian population in northern Iraq in August 1933. The term is not only used to describe the Simele massacre but also the broader genocidal campaign that took place in over a hundred Assyrian villages in Dohuk and Nineveh, resulting in the deaths of over six thousand Assyrians. Despite the establishment of the Iraqi state in 1932, the Assyrians continued their quest for statehood, appealing to the League of Nations for autonomy, protection, and guarantees of freedom to emigrate from Iraq in the event of massacres against them. Public animosity towards the Assyrians was widespread, as Iraqi nationalist propaganda campaigns had portrayed them as violent rebels, and Iraqi officials had defamed them. The anticipated violence against the Assyrians began in August 1933. Iraqi troops, joined by marauders from Kurdish tribes, orchestrated a massacre of hundreds of Assyrian civilians in northern Iraq and pillaged their villages. The Assyrians resisted the attacks, and the town of Simele became a haven for Assyrians fleeing the targeted areas. General Bakr Sidqi, an Iraqi nationalist of Kurdish origin, received government permission to eliminate "all Assyrians." The Assyrians in Simele were forcibly disarmed before Iraqi troops and Kurdish irregulars arrived in the district without warning or provocation, opening fire indiscriminately on the defenseless Assyrians. Some Assyrian women were mutilated. The residents of 65 Assyrian villages were massacred, with up to 3,000 in Simele, where it is said the "worst massacres of all" occurred. Reports began to emerge that even nine-year-old girls were being raped and burned alive. Most of the children were stabbed to death while throwing themselves onto the headless, lifeless bodies of their mothers. The violent Iraqi campaign against its indigenous community persisted until August 16, 1933, but violent raids against the Assyrians continued until the end of the month. The Assyrians were largely confined to their homes out of fear of further attacks. According to an eyewitness account by Lieutenant Colonel Ronald Sempill Stafford, the British administrative inspector of Mosul: "Here and there in the mountains, they encounter fleeing

Assyrians. And every Assyrian they captured they shot to kill, without any mercy." Evidently, by now the army had decided that the Assyrians, as far as possible, would be exterminated. No claim was made that these operations had a purely military objective, as army intelligence officers did not even bother to interrogate the captured Assyrians, who were simply gunned down as they were gathered. It was now evident that the Army Command was quite certain in its mind that, in its decision to wipe out the Assyrians, it would be supported not only by Arab public opinion but by the government in Baghdad. A total of 6,000 Assyrian men, women, and children were massacred, while tens of thousands more were forcibly displaced. Thousands of women have been sexually assaulted, many of them kidnapped, with no trace of their whereabouts. Those who escaped the violence survived only to live in a state of hunger and complete marginalization. The Simele massacre, which closely followed the Assyrian genocide, marked the end of the Assyrian quest for a homeland. The Iraqi government has never acknowledged the Simele massacre, despite appeals from Assyrian representatives. Additionally, the Assyrians who were killed in the events of 1933 were callously buried in mass graves. Family members of the victims were barred from exhuming the bodies for a proper burial. The mass grave from the 1933 Simele Massacre is presently identified by a sign bearing the inscription "Simele Archaeological Hill" atop a substantial, barren hill. The bones of the Simele Massacre victims are strewn across the site, jutting from the earth and laid bare for onlookers. The area remains unprotected, treated as a refuse dump, and is frequently strewn with garbage. The regional government of Kurdistan has also erected a communications tower atop the hill, which the Assyrians find offensive. Assyrians have long sought a dignified burial and proper commemoration at the site, but it continues to be neglected.

The massacre of the Assyrians in Soriya

On the morning of September 16, 1969, Iraqi forces led by Lieutenant Abdul Karim al-Jahayshee attacked the Assyrian village of Soriya, located in Dohuk, Iraq. Over a hundred Assyrians inhabited the village during the assault. Forty-seven village residents were killed, including the local village priest, and twenty-two were injured. According to the eyewitness account of a survivor: "I was ten years old and fell to the ground. A woman fell on top of me, and her blood covered me. Other children were also covered in blood and presumed dead." At the same time, Iraqi army soldiers in our village began to scatter, shooting into houses and setting them on fire. As we ran, some fleeing with us fell to the ground from gunshot wounds, bleeding to death. We were all running towards the village of Bakhlogia, four kilometers away, to take cover. We reached Bakhlogia, but the villagers could not provide us refuge; it was too dangerous. Although the exact motivation behind the Soriya massacre remains unknown, the intention was clear. The massacre is believed to have occurred in response to a mine detonated beneath a military vehicle near the village during a time when the Assyrians were actively involved in armed resistance against the ruling Ba'ath Party. The Iraqi government has never acknowledged the Soriya massacre, and there is very little research on the subject.

Genocide and Ethnic Cleansing at the Hands of ISIS

In 2014, the ISIS advance into Iraq's Nineveh Plains devastated the indigenous Assyrian community in the region, as hundreds of thousands of people were forcibly displaced. There were a small number of Assyrian casualties, and some Assyrian women were taken captive by the terrorist group to be sold as sex slaves. At the time of the ISIS advance, the Peshmerga forces[23] of the Kurdistan Regional Government (KRG) were responsible for maintaining security in the region. Nevertheless, following the disarmament of the local Assyrians, the Peshmerga preemptively retreated from these areas prior to the ISIS attack, failing to notify the local populations. Left vulnerable, the Assyrians and

---

[23] The Peshmerga (in Kurdish, Pêşmerge, literally "before death") are the armed forces of the autonomous region of Iraqi Kurdistan. The term "Peshmerga" literally signifies a fighter-guerrilla who is prepared to battle to the death.

other ethnic communities in the Nineveh Plain were compelled to escape. According to the account of an Assyrian man from the city of Bakhdida: "It was around 3 in the afternoon. I was driving with a friend when we heard an explosion nearby. We headed in that direction to see what had happened. We could hear people screaming as we got closer. Two children, aged six and eight, who were playing soccer, were hit by a mortar. That is when we realized that ISIS was on its way. We gathered their remains and placed them in an empty potato chip bag, which we then handed over to their families. We realized that the Peshmerga had abandoned us overnight. Word spread quickly, and then the church bells rang, a signal that it was time to leave. We did not know if we would make it in time. No human should experience this kind of terror. The ISIS assault led to the expulsion and effective exile of the Assyrian people from their ancestral lands. While the vast majority of Assyrians managed to escape the imminent violence, nearly half of the displaced did not return. This campaign of ethnic cleansing against the Assyrians coincided with the horrific Yazidi genocide[24] in Sinjar, during which approximately 5,000 people were killed, with thousands of women abducted and subjected to sexual slavery. The atrocities committed by ISIS against Yazidis and Christians have been officially recognized as genocide by the United Nations, the European Parliament, and a number of individual nations. The United States House of Representatives and the U.S. Department of State recognized the genocide in 2016. In February 2015, ISIS launched an assault on the 35 Assyrian villages in the Khabour region of Syria. Numerous lives were claimed in the attack, and over 200 Assyrian civilians were seized by the terrorist group. The villages were plundered and left in ruins. While the majority of the captives were eventually released, three of them were ruthlessly murdered on camera in a video that was made public online. Tragically, most of the Assyrians in the Khabour region during the ISIS attack period had either survived the 1933 Simele massacre or were their descendants. The events of 2015 led to the expulsion and effective exile of

---

[24] Originally hailing from the northern regions of present-day Iraq, the Yazidis have recently garnered international attention as among the most heavily victimized by ISIS between 2014 and 2015.

the Assyrian people from an area they had inhabited almost exclusively for nearly a century. "This is the fate of the Assyrians," said a woman who survived the February 2015 attacks in Khabour. "My grandmother used to tell me stories of the [Assyrian] genocide." I never thought that one day I would have a story like this to tell," the narrator said. In addition to murder, enslavement, and sexual exploitation of tens of thousands of Yazidis, Assyrians, and other victims, ISIS's policy of genocide and ethnic cleansing also involved the deliberate destruction of the Yazidi and Assyrian cultural heritage.

The effects of genocide outlast the violence. Some of the enduring impacts of the genocide on the Assyrian people include:

The lives of millions of Assyrians were lost or destroyed;

The expropriation and destruction of Assyrian lands and the enforced demographic change in regions historically inhabited by the Assyrians;

The forced and often permanent separation of Assyrian families, a trend that continues to this day due to ongoing persecutions;

The ruin and disintegration of Assyrian social and religious structures;

The end of the Assyrian quest for statehood; The forced dispersal of the Assyrian population across newly formed nation-states, creating enduring divisions among the Assyrian people;

The fragmentation, marginalization, and subjugation of the Assyrians to hostile governments;

The expropriation of Assyrian ethnic identity and the forced assimilation into dominant cultures, namely, Arabization, Turkification, and Kurdification;

The destruction of Assyrian cultural heritage, including buildings, books, artworks, and artifacts;

The obstruction of accurate documentation of modern Assyrian history;

Transgenerational trauma and profound psychological effects among those directly and indirectly exposed to genocidal violence;

The successive "lost generations" of Assyrians;

The persistent existential threat that the Assyrian people continue to confront in the present.

Monuments

The only governments that have allowed the Assyrians to erect monuments to commemorate the victims of the Assyrian genocide are France, Australia, Sweden, Armenia, Belgium, and the United States. The Swedish government has committed to covering all expenses for a future monument, following strong advocacy from the large Assyrian community, led by politician Konstantin Sabo. There are three monuments in the United States, one in Chicago, one in Columbus, and the most recent one in Los Angeles, California.

Recent reports suggest that Armenia is prepared to establish a monument dedicated to the Assyrian genocide, to be located in the capital city alongside the Armenian genocide memorial.

A monument to the victims of the Assyrian genocide has been erected in Fairfield, Australia, a suburb of Sydney where ten percent of the population is of Assyrian descent. The statue is crafted in the form of a martyr's hand draped in an Assyrian flag and stands at 4.5 meters tall. It was designed by Lewis Batros, an Australian artist of Assyrian origin. The memorial is situated in a reserve to be named the Garden of Nineveh. The commemorative statue and the reserve's name were proposed in August 2009 by the Assyrian Universal Alliance. After consulting the community, the Fairfield Council received over a hundred requests for the memorial, some of which came from overseas, along with two petitions. The proposal faced opposition from the Australian Turkish community. The Assyrian genocide has gained recognition from the local government of New South Wales and the state of South Australia. On August 30, 2010, just twenty-three days after its inauguration, the Australian monument was vandalized.

In 2013, a monument to the Assyrian genocide was unveiled in Belgium. The monument features a dove, symbolizing peace. There are also other Assyrian genocide memorials in France, Russia, and Armenia. In Canada, the Assyrian genocide, along with the Armenian genocide, is covered in a course on historical genocides. Turkish organizations, along with other non-Turkish Muslim organizations, have reacted negatively, as is often the case, by protesting.

Conclusions

Assyrians have struggled to preserve the oral histories of their early 20th-century families and pass those memories on to other communities and future generations. However, they have been hindered in this by a lack of access to print, television stations, academic centers, and websites. Even when their work is published, they encounter pressures to reconcile it with conventional wisdom. When the contemporary political situation of Assyrians is raised, the objection may be that there is no connection to historical tragedies. This stands in stark contrast to the ordinary work of Middle East studies and genocide studies, which explicitly links the contemporary politics of many nations to their histories. The Assyrians represent a unique case in history, as a population that has repeatedly been denied the recognized claim of distinct ethnic, national, and religious continuity with their ancestors. It is believed that the history of the Christians in Hakkari and Urmia has no moral or legal implications for today's policies towards Turkey and Iran, or for the legal status of their laws or national boundaries, just as the history of Muslims in Jerusalem or Sarajevo, for example, is considered highly significant in shaping policies towards Israel or the former Yugoslavia. Securing recognition of the Assyrian genocide has been a significant challenge due to the absence of national support institutions, the small number of Assyrians remaining worldwide, and the efforts of various powerful nation-states to downplay and justify the tragedy. The concept of genocide, coined by Lemkin and adopted by the United Nations, is fitting for the eradication of a national and religious group from most of its historical homeland, resulting in decimation and dispersal.

179

Assyrians have been struggling for over a hundred years to convey the extent of their national, ethnic, and religious decline to a generally indifferent world.

Convention of December 9, 1948 for the Prevention and Punishment of the Crime of Genocide

Concluded in New York on December 9, 1948 Approved by the Federal Assembly on March 9, 2002 Ratified with instruments deposited on September 7, 2000 Entered into force for Switzerland on December 6, 2000

The High Contracting Parties,

considering that the United Nations General Assembly, in Resolution 96 (1) of December 11, 1946, declared genocide to be a crime under international law, contrary to the spirit and purposes of the United Nations and condemned by the civilized world;

recognizing that genocide, throughout all historical epochs, has inflicted serious losses on humanity; convinced that international cooperation is necessary to rid humanity of such a heinous scourge, agree as follow:

Article I

The Contracting Parties confirm that genocide, whether committed in times of peace or in times of war, is a crime under international law that they undertake to prevent and punish.

Article II

In this Convention, genocide means each of the following acts committed with the intent to destroy, in whole or in part, a national, ethnic, racial, or religious group as such:

a) Killing members of the group;

b) Causing serious bodily or mental harm to members of the group;

c) Deliberately imposing conditions of life intended to bring about the physical, total, or partial destruction of the group;

d) Implementing measures to prevent births within the group;

e) Forcibly transferring children from one group to another.

Article III

The following acts shall be punishable:

a) Genocide;

b) Conspiracy to commit genocide;

c) Direct and public incitement to commit genocide;

d) Attempt to commit genocide;

e) Complicity in genocide.

Article IV

Persons who commit genocide or any of the acts listed in Article III shall be punished, whether they hold the status of constitutionally responsible rulers or are public officials or private individuals.

Article V

The Contracting Parties commit to enacting, in accordance with their respective Constitutions, the necessary laws to implement the provisions of this Convention, particularly to establish effective criminal penalties for individuals guilty of genocide or any of the other acts listed in Article III.

Article VI

Persons accused of genocide or any of the other acts listed in Article III shall be tried by the competent courts of the State in whose territory the act was committed, or by the relevant international criminal tribunal with jurisdiction recognized by those contracting parties.

Article VII

Genocide and the other acts listed in Article III shall not be considered as political crimes for the purposes of extradition. The contracting parties commit, in such cases, to grant extradition in accordance with their laws and the treaties in force.

Article VIII

Each contracting party may invite the competent bodies of the United Nations to take, in accordance with the United Nations Charter, any measures they deem appropriate for the purpose of preventing and suppressing acts of genocide or any of the other acts listed in Article III.

Article IX

Disputes between the contracting parties concerning the interpretation, application, or execution of this Convention, including those related to the responsibility of a State for acts of genocide or any of the other acts listed in Article III, shall be submitted to the International Court of Justice upon the request of one of the parties to the dispute.

Article X

This Convention, of which the Chinese, English, French, Russian, and Spanish texts are equally authentic, shall bear the date of December 9, 1948.

Article XI

This Convention shall be open for signature by every Member of the United Nations and by every non-member State to which the General Assembly has extended an invitation for this purpose until December 31, 1949. This Convention shall be ratified, and the instruments of ratification shall be deposited with the Secretary-General of the United Nations. From January 1, 1950, any Member of the United Nations and any non-member State that has received the aforementioned invitation may accede to this Convention. The instruments of accession shall be deposited with the Secretary-General of the United Nations.

Article XII

Any contracting party may, at any time, by notification addressed to the Secretary-General of the United Nations, extend the application of this Convention to all territories or any of the territories for which it directs its foreign relations.

Article XIII

On the day when the first twenty instruments of ratification or accession have been deposited, the Secretary-General shall draw up a procès-verbal and transmit a copy of it to each Member of the United Nations and to each of the non-member States referred to in Article XI. This Convention shall enter into force on the ninetieth day following the date of deposit of the twentieth instrument of ratification or accession. Any ratification or accession made subsequent to that date shall take effect on the ninetieth day following the deposit of the instrument of ratification or accession.

Article XIV

This Convention shall have a duration of ten years from its entry into force. Thereafter, it shall remain in force for successive periods of five years among those contracting parties that have not denounced it at least six months prior to the expiration of the term. Denunciation shall be made by written notification addressed to the Secretary-General of the United Nations.

Article XV

If, as a result of denunciations, the number of parties to this Convention becomes less than sixteen, the Convention shall cease to be in force from the date on which the last of such denunciations becomes effective.

Article XVI

At any time, any contracting party may initiate a request for the revision of this Convention by means of a written notification addressed to the Secretary-General. The General Assembly shall determine the measures to be taken, if any, regarding such request.

Article XVII

The Secretary-General of the United Nations shall notify all Members of the United Nations and the non-member States referred to in Article XI:

a) the signatures, ratifications, and accessions received in accordance with Article XI;

b) the notifications received in accordance with Article XII;

c) the date on which this Convention shall enter into force, in accordance with Article XIII;

d) the denunciations received in accordance with Article XIV;

e) the abrogation of the Convention, in accordance with Article XV;

f) the notifications received in accordance with Article XVI.

Article XVIII

The original of this Convention shall be deposited in the archives of the United Nations. A certified true copy shall be sent to all Members of the United Nations and to all non-member States referred to in Article XI.

Art. XIX

This Convention shall be registered by the Secretary-General of the United Nations on the date of its entry into force.

Bibliography and Sources

In English

Abrahamian, Ervand. *Iran between Two Revolutions* (Princeton: Princeton UniversityPress, 1982).

Allen, Henry Elisha. *The Turkish Transformation: A Study in Social and Religious Development* (Westport, CT: Greenwood Press, 1968).

Amery, Leo. "Question of the Frontier between Turkey and Iraq," *League of Nations Official Journal* 6 (1925): 1440–1441, 1440.

Anzerlioğlu, Yonca. "The Revolts of Nestorian Christians against the Ottoman Empire and the Republic of Turkey," *The Muslim World* 100, no. 1 (2010): 45–59.

Armenian Assembly of America, Inc. *European Court of Human Rights Rules in Favor of Armenian Genocide Scholar Taner Akcam; Court Finds Article 301 of the Turkish Penal Code Violates European Convention on Human Rights* (Oct. 25, 2011)

Associated Press. "Mosul Awarded to British; More Turk Killings Alleged," *The Washington Post* (Dec. 16, 1925), 1.

Atto, Naures. *Hostages in the Homeland, Orphans in the Diaspora: Identity Discourses among the Assyrian/Syriac Elites in the European Diaspora* (Leiden: Leiden University Press, 2011).

Balakian, Peter. *The Burning Tigris: The Armenian Genocide and America's Response* (New York: HarperCollins, 2003).

Barkey, Karen. "The Ottoman Millet System: Non-Territorial Autonomy and Its Contemporary Legacy," *Ethnopolitics* 15 (2016): 24–42.

Baum, Wilhelm. *The Christian Minorities in Turkey: History-Genocide-Presence* (Leverkusen: Kitap Verlag, 2005).

Bjørnlund, Matthias. "The 1914 Cleansing of Aegean Greeks as a Case of Violent Turkification," *Journal of Genocide Research* 10, no. 1 (2008); 41–57.

Bleachler, Donald. *The Genocide Debate: Politicians, Academic, and Victims* (London: Springer, 2011).

Bloxham, Donald. *Genocide, the World Wars, and the Unweaving of Europe* (Portland, OR: Valentine Mitchell, 2005).

Bostom, Andrew. *The Legacy of Jihad* (Amherst, NY: Prometheus Books, 2010).

Boyajian, Dickran. *Armenia: The Case for a Forgotten Genocide* (Westwood, NJ: Educational Bookcrafters, 1972).

Butcher, Kevin. *Roman Syria and the Near East* (London: The British Museum and Los Angeles, CA: Getty Publications, 2003).

Campo, Juan Eduardo (Ed.). *Encyclopedia of Islam* (New York: Infobase Publishing, 2009), 703.

Canard, Marius. *L'Expansion arabo-islamique et ses répercussions*, vol. 6 (London: Variorum Reprints, 1974).

Carty, Anthony. "The Iraq Invasion as a Recent United Kingdom 'Contribution to International Law'," *European Journal of International Law* 16 (2005): 143–151.

Catherwood, Christopher and Leslie Ann Horvitz. *Encyclopedia of War Crimes and Genocide* (New York: Facts on File, 2006).

Center for Jewish History. *Raphael Lemkin Papers* (2012), http://tinyurl.com/lemkin papers.

Dadrian, Vahakn. "The Documentation of the Armenian Genocide in German and Austrian Sources," in Israel Charny and Alan L. Berger (Eds.), *The Widening Circle of Genocide* (New Brunswick, NJ: Transaction, 1994), 103–124.

Donabed, Sargon. *Reforging a Forgotten History: Iraq and the Assyrians in the 20th Century* (Edinburgh: University of Edinburgh Press, 2015).
Ehteshami, Anoushiravan and Emma Murphy. *The International Politics of the Red Sea* (Abingdon and New York: Routledge, 2013).

Falk, Richard. "Foreword: The Armenian Genocide in Official Turkish Records," *Journal of Political and Military Sociology* 22, no. 1 (1994): 1–2.

Gaunt, David with Jan-Bet Sawoce and Racho Donef. *Massacres, Resistance, Protectors: Muslim-Christian relations in Eastern Anatolia during World War I* (Piscataway, NJ: Gorgias Press, 2006).

Gorder, Christian van. *Armenian Christians and Turkish Muslims: Atrocity, Denial and Identity* (2004), www.samford.edu/lillyhumanrights/papers/VanGorder_Armenian. pdf.

Gust, Wolfgang. *The Armenian Genocide: Evidence from the German Foreign Office Archives 1915–1916* (New York: Berghahn Books, 2013).

Halo, Thea. *Not Even My Name: From a Death March in Turkey to a New Home in America, a Young Girl's True Story* (New York: St. Martin's, 2000/2001). Hannibal Travis, The assyrian genocide, New York, 2018

Hourani, Albert. *Minorities in the Arab World* (Oxford: Oxford University Press, 1947).

Itano, Nicole. "Why Armenia Pays High Price for 'Genocide' Campaign," *The Christian Science Monitor* (Apr. 23, 2007).

Jacobs, Steven. *Lemkin on Genocide: Written by Raphael Lemkin* (Lanham, MD: Lexington Books, 2012).

James, Edwin. "Kemal Won't Insure against Massacres," *New York Times* (Sept. 11, 1922), in Kostos, *Before the Silence*, 183.

Jones, Adam. *Genocide: A Comprehensive Introduction* (Abingdon and New York: Routledge, 2nd ed., 2010).

Katz, Steven. *The Holocaust in Historical Context: The Holocaust and Mass Death before the Modern Age*, vol. 1 (Oxford: Oxford University Press, 1994).

Kefeli, Agnes. *Becoming Muslim in Imperial Russia: Conversion, Apostasy, and Literacy* (Ithaca, NY: Cornell University Press, 2014).

Kévorkian, Raymond. *Armenian Genocide, The: A Complete History* (London: I.B. Tauris, 2011).

Klein, Janet. *The Margins of Empire: Kurdish Militias in the Ottoman Tribal Zone* (Palo Alto, CA: Stanford University Press, 2011).

Laing-Marshall, Andrea. *Modern Assyrian Identity and the Church of the East: An Exploration of their Relationship and the Rise of Assyrian Nationalism, From the World Wars to 1980*, M.A. Thesis, Toronto School of Theology, 2001.

Lemkin, Raphael. *Axis Rule in Occupied Europe: Laws of Occupation – Analysis of Government – Proposals for Redress* (Washington, DC: Carnegie Endowment for International Peace, 1943)
———. *Dossier on the Armenian Genocide*, ed. Michael Bazyler (Glendale, CA: Center for Armenian Remembrance, 2008).

———. *Raphael Lemkin Collection, Box 9, Folder 2, Armenians and Assyrians,* undated (The Assyrian

Case, Notecard 39–47) (1948?), Center for Jewish History Digital Collections.

Levene, Mark. "Book Review (David Gaunt, *Massacres, Resistance, Protectors: Muslim-Christian Relations in Eastern Anatolia during World War I*)," *Journal of Genocide Research* 10, no. 1 (2008): 155–182.
———. "Creating a Modern 'Zone of Genocide': The Impact of Nation- and State-
Formation on Eastern Anatolia, 1878–1923," *Holocaust and Genocide Studies* 12 (1998): 398–411.
———. *Devastation: Volume I: The European Rimlands 1912–1938* (Oxford: Oxford University Press, 2013).
———. *Genocide in the Age of the Nation-State: The Rise of the West and the Coming of Genocide* (London: I.B. Tauris, 2005).
———. "A Moving Target, the Usual Suspects and (Maybe) a Smoking Gun: The Problem of Pinning Blame in Modern Genocide," *Patterns of Prejudice* 3 (1999): 3–24.

Lewy, Guenter. *The Armenian Massacres in Ottoman Turkey: A Disputed Genocide* (Salt Lake City: University of Utah Press, 2005).

Maclean, Arthur John. *A Dictionary of the Dialects of Vernacular Syriac: As Spoken by the Eastern Syrians of Kurdistan, North-West Persia, and the Plain of Mosul* (Oxford: Clarendon Press, 1901).

Mangasarian, M.M. "'Armenia's Impending Doom: Our Duty," reprinted in Arman Kirakosian (Ed.), *The Armenian Massacres, 1894–1896: U.S. Media Testimony* (Detroit: Wayne State University Press, 2004), 164–175.

Marashlian, Levon. *Politics and Demography: Armenians, Turks and Kurds in the Ottoman Empire* (Toronto, Canada: Zoryan Institute, 1990).

Melson, Robert. *Revolution and Genocide: On the Origins of the Armenian Genocide and the Holocaust* (Chicago: University of Chicago Press, 1992).

Milner, Thomas. *The Ottoman Empire: The Sultans, the Territory, and the People* (London: The Religious Tract Society, 1799).

Morgenthau, Henry. *Ambassador Morgenthau's Story* (New York and Garden City: Doubleday, 1919).

Naayem, Joseph. *Shall This Nation Die?* (New York: Chaldean Rescue, 1921).

Nogales, Rafael de. *Four Years Beneath the Crescent*, trans. Muna Lee (New York: C. Scribner's Sons, 1926).

Quataert, Donald. *The Ottoman Empire 1700–1912* (Cambridge: Cambridge University Press, 2005).

Reynolds, Michael. *Shattering Empires: The Clash and Collapse of the Ottoman and Russian Empires* (Cambridge: Cambridge University Press, 2011).

Rollinger, Robert. "The Terms 'Assyria' and 'Syria' Again," *Journal of Near Eastern Studies* 65, no. 4 (2006): 284–287.

Samur, Hakan. "Turkey's Europeanization Process and the Return of the Syriacs," *Turkish Studies* 10, no. 3 (2009): 327–340.

Schabas, William. *Genocide in International Law: The Crime of Crimes* (Cambridge: Cambridge University Press, 2000).

Schneider, Adam and Selim Adali. "'No Harvest Was Reaped': Demographic and Climatic Factors in the Decline of the Neo-Assyrian Empire," *Climatic Change* 127, no. 3 (2014): 435–446.

Shahbaz, Yonan. *The Rage of Islam: An Account of the Massacre of Christians by the Turks in Persia* (Philadelphia: Roger Williams Press, 1918).

Shaw, Stafford and Ezel Kural Shaw. *History of the Ottoman Empire and Modern Turkey*, vol. 2 (Cambridge: Cambridge University Press, 1977).

Sonyel, Salâhi. *The Assyrians of Turkey. Victims of Major Power Policy* (Ankara: Turkish Historical Society, 2001).

Stafford, Lt. Col. Ronald. *The Tragedy of the Assyrians* (London: Kegan Paul, 1935).

Toynbee, Arnold. "A Summary of Armenian History up to and Including the Year 1915," in Ara Sarafian (Ed.), *The Treatment of Armenians in the Ottoman Empire, 1915–1916: Documents Presented to the Viscount Grey of Fallod on* (Reading, UK: Taderon Press, 2000), 34–35.

————. *The Western Question in Greece and Turkey* (London: Constable, 1923).

Travis, Hannibal. "The Assyrian Genocide: A Tale of Oblivion and Denial," in Rene Lemarchand (Ed.), *Forgotten Genocides: Oblivion, Genocide, and Denial* (Philadelphia: University of Pennsylvania Press, 2011), 123–136.

Trumpener, Ulrich. *Germany and the Ottoman Empire, 1914–1918* (Princeton, NJ: Princeton University Press, 1968).

Walker, Christopher. *Armenia: The Survival of a Nation* (New York: St. Martin's Press, 2nd ed., 1990).

Willcox, Sir William. "Mesopotamia," in *The Encyclopedia Britannica* (New York: Encyclopedia Britannica, 1922).

Wilmshurst, David. *The Martyred Church: A History of the Church of the East* (Sawbridgeworth, Hertfordshire: East & West Publishing, 2011).

Yohannan, Abraham. *The Death of a Nation: Or the EverPersecuted Nestorians or Assyrian Christians* (New York: G.P. Putnam's Sons, 1916).

In Italian

Valentina Vartui Karakhanian, O. Viganò, *La Santa Sede e lo Sterminio degli Armeni nell'Impero Ottomano. Dai documenti dell'Archivio Segreto Vaticano e dell'Archivio Storico della Segreteria di Stato*, Milano, Guerini e Associati, 2016

Nora Arissian, *Il genocidio armeno 1915. Nel pensiero degli intellettuali arabi siriani*, prefazione, traduzione e cura di Kegham J. Boloyan, Bari, Radici Future, 2018

Henry Barby, *Nella Terra del Terrore: Il Martirio dell'Armenia*, a cura di Carlo Coppola, presentazione di Sargis Ghazaryan, Bari, LB edizioni, 2016

Aghavni Boghosian, *Il richiamo del sangue. Ricordi... dal genocidio armeno 1915*, introduzione e cura di Kegham J. Boloyan, traduzione dall'arabo di S. Coletta e K. J. Boloyan, FaL Vision, Bari 2012 (tit. orig. *Nida' ad-Damm*, Casa Editrice Cilicia, Aleppo 1998)

Gilbert Sinoué, *Armenia*, Neri Pozza Editore, 2011

Hrant Dink, *L'inquietudine della colomba. Essere armeni in Turchia*, Milano, Guerini e associati, 2008

Marcello Flores, *Il genocidio degli armeni*, Bologna, Il Mulino, 2007

Alberto Rosselli, *L'olocausto armeno*, ed. Solfanelli, 2007

Guenter Lewy, *Il massacro degli armeni*, Torino, Einaudi, 2006

Diego Cimara, *Il genocidio turco degli armeni*, Treviso, Editing, 2006

Taner Akçam, *Nazionalismo turco e genocidio armeno. Dall'Impero ottomano alla Repubblica*, Milano, Guerini e associati, 2005

N. Dadrian Vahakn, *Storia del genocidio armeno. Conflitti nazionali dai Balcani al Caucaso*, ed. Guerini e associati, 2003

Yves Ternon, *Gli Armeni. 1915-1916: il genocidio dimenticato*, Rizzoli, 2003

Hrand Nazariantz, *L'Armenia, il suo martirio e le sue rivendicazioni*, con introduzione di Giorgio D'Acandia (pseud. di Umberto Zanotti Bianco), Battiato, Catania 1916

Ivan Maffei, *Giustizia per gli armeni. Il processo Tehlirian: analisi e implicazioni politiche*, Youcanprint, 2021

In Spanish

Armenia (Jean P.Alem) Buenos Aires, 1963,

Armenia. 90° Aniversario del genocidio armenio (Armenian Cultural Association).

Armenia y la cuestión armenia (Simón Vratzian) Library of the La Plata University.

Armenia y la causa armenia (H.Thorosian) Buenos Aires, 1995.

Armin T.Wegner: polémica por los derechos humanos de armenios y judíos (Sybil Milton) Ierevan, 1990.

Cuatro años bajo la Media Luna (Raphael de Nogales) Buenos Aires, 1924.

El genocidio armenio. Su interrelación con el holocausto judío (Rita C. Kuyumciyan) Buenos Aires, 2006.

El derrumbre del negacionismo. Leandro Despouy, el informe Whitaker y otros (Khatchik Derghougassian (comp.) Buenos Aires, 2009.

El genocidio armenio en la prensa argentina (Nélida Boulgourdjian) Buenos Aires, 2005.

El mercado de esclavas de Kemal y el tratado de Lausana. El turco no ha cambiado (William T.Manning) United States, 1924.

El primer genocidio del siglo XX. Regreso de la memoria armenia (Rita C.Kuyumciyan) Buenos Aires. 2009.

El grito armenio: crónica de un genocidio y lucha por su reconocimiento (Mariano Saravia, Osvaldo Bayer) Córdoba, 2007.

El genocidio contra los armenios (Alfred de Zayas) Buenos Aires, 2009.

El Estado criminal. Los genocidas en el siglo XX (Yves Ternon) Barcelona, 1995.

El genocidio contra los armenios. 1915-1923, with a prologue by the International Commission of Jurists (Alfred de Zayas) Buenos Aires, 2009.

Historia del pueblo armenio (Ashod Artzruni) La Plata University Library.

La cuestión armenia y las relaciones internacionales (Pascual Ohanian) Buenos Aires. 1994.

Le rapport secret sur les massacres d'Arméniem (Johannes Lepsius) París, 1918.

Les massacres en Arménie turque (Faiz el Hussein) Bombay, 1917.

Los determinantes del genocidio armenio (Vahakn N. Dadrián) Buenos Aires, 1999.

Los factores comunes en dos genocides (Vahakn N. Dadrián) Buenos Aires, 2005.

Los elementos claves en el negacionismo turco del genocidio armenio (Vahakn N. Dadrián) Buenos Aires 2002.

Los armenios. ¿El primer negacionismo del siglo XX? (Guenter Lewy) EE.UU. 2005.

Los armenios. Retrato de una esperanza (Huberta von Voss) Buenos Aires, 2007.

Los armenios en la Argentina (Eva Tabakian) La Plata University Library.

Los cuarenta días del Musa Dagh (Franz Werfel) Buenos Aires, 2004.

Memorias (Henry Morgenthau) Buenos Aires, 1975.

Newspapers: Armenia, Clarín, La Nación, Página/12; Magazine: Realidad Económica. Internet.

Responsabilidad alemana en el genocidio armenio (Vahakn N.Dadrian) Massachusetts, 1996.

Seis estudios sobre genocidio (Daniel Feierstein) Buenos Aires, 2000.

Sulim Granowsky, El genocidio silenciado, ed. Continente, Buenos Aires, 2014.

Una visión desde Uruguay: el genocidio armenio noventa años después (Coriún Aharonián) Brecha, Uruguay, 1995

Summary